D1249297

MELVIN J. MAAS,

Gallant Man of Action

Men of Achievement

Other Books in the Men of Achievement Series:

Herbert Hoover, Humanitarian
Ernest Hemingway, Man of Courage
Conrad N. Hilton, Hotelier
J. Edgar Hoover, Modern Knight Errant
Dr. Albert Schweitzer, Medical Missionary
Carl Sandburg, Poet and Patriot
Lowell Thomas, Adventurer
Charles F. Kettering, Inventor and Idealist
Bob Mathias, Champion of Champions
Frank H. Krusen, M.D., Pioneer in Physical Medicine and Rehabilitation
J. C. Penney, Merchant Prince
Nathaniel Leverone, Pioneer in Automatic Merchandising
Harry A. Bullis, Champion American
John Foster Dulles, Peacemaker
William L. McKnight, Industrialist
Lyndon B. Johnson, Man of Reason
Norman Vincent Peale, Christian Crusader
General Carlos P. Romulo, Defender of Freedom
Edgar James Helms, the Goodwill Man
Hubert H. Humphrey, Champion of Human Rights
John J. Brousch, Conqueror of Adversity
Frank C. Laubach, Teacher of Millions
Oscar Winchell, Alaska's Flying Cowboy

Men of Achievement Series

MELVIN J. MAAS,
Gallant Man of Action

By

GLADYS ZEHNPFENNIG

Publishers
T. S. DENISON & COMPANY, INC.
Minneapolis

Printed in the U. S. A.
By THE BRINGS PRESS

Library of Congress Catalog Card Number: 67-21407

To Sergeant Gary Zehnpfennig
and all the other young Marines
who have taken the long, long trail
from Pendleton to Okinawa to South Vietnam.

Foreword

The achievement record of Major Gen. Melvin J. Maas resembles a kaleidoscope. No matter how you shake it up, it falls into patterns that retain their vivid, exciting sparkle.

He was not a tall man, but he was deliberately "larger than life" in his thoughts and deeds. He had an ageless quality about him. In another century, he might have been an armored knight, a buccaneering explorer, or even a Francis of Assisi. Whatever he chose to do, it would be dramatic. There would be gallantry and a special flair and flavor to it.

When a deranged man threatened the House of Representatives with a loaded revolver, did Congressman Maas dash for an exit? When his colleagues scoffed at his assertion that a one-man aerial bombardment could wipe out the national government, did he put on a demonstration? When he learned that he might soon become alarmingly disabled, did he collapse and give up the struggle? General Maas is a "Man of Achievement" because he always did the unpredictable.

Mel was not content merely to exist; he wanted to live to the utmost, with laughter and good fellowship and plenty of "active duty." In all of his dynamic "lives," he shunned mediocrity. When he hopped into the cockpit of a plane, he was a swashbuckling pilot in the grand tradition. It was typical that Maas—a Marine Colonel—should come home from the South Pacific during World War II with an Army Silver Star from General Douglas MacArthur.

A Republican, Mel Maas won the respect and admiration of colleagues of both parties. On the floor of Congress, and in Congressional and Defense Committee meetings, he was a statesman of eloquence and wit. His Guam debates in the House will continue to be significant for many decades to come.

Even after he suffered a major physical disability, he plunged into the years of darkness ahead with high good humor. He faced his problem squarely and re-educated himself to lead a vibrantly useful life. As Chairman of the President's Committee on Employment of the Handicapped, he inspired millions of other victims of tragedy all over the world to look toward the future with renewed faith and hope. Mel Maas demonstrated, over and over again, that he had one of the most "undaunted" personalities in the history of mankind.

This book will be of particular interest to high school students who may soon be entering the armed forces. In addition to everything else, General Maas was a key figure in the drafting of the Ready Reserve and Standby Reserve programs.

Contents

Introduction

One of the most overworked cliches in the English language is the characterization of the life of a deceased person as an "inspiration" to his contemporaries and those who follow him. Nevertheless, each generation does produce some exceptional men and women who, through the selfless example they set, merit this high tribute. One such person was Melvin J. Maas.

Mel Maas and I became friends while serving together in the U. S. House of Representatives. There existed the added bond of having served in the Marines, although I must admit that an examination of our military careers would show considerable disparity: his ultimate rank of general eclipsed my personal career zenith as private first class.

As a Congressman, as a Marine officer, and later in life as the chairman of the President's Committee on Employment of the Handicapped, Mel Maas displayed the highest personal courage. He showed it in facing down a mentally disturbed gunman who terrorized the House of Representatives. He showed it repeatedly in the Pacific during World War II where he received several decorations.

But the crowning achievement of Mel Maas' life has to be the way he accepted the personal tragedy of blindness and forged a new career at an age when most people would lie down and quit. Although suffering from the combined afflictions of blindness, several heart attacks, an ulcerated stomach, diabetes, arthritis, and a host of lesser ailments, Mel Maas was going full tilt when he died. His example was indeed an "inspiration" to all who knew him.

In this highly readable and entertaining account of Mel Maas, Mrs. Zehnpfennig has captured the essence of the man. This is no easy task when you have a subject who, at one moment, is "buzzing" the House of Representatives by private plane during a State-of-the-Union speech to prove that the government of the United States could be put out of existence with a single bomb, and at the next moment is down to earth displaying his deep compassion for the sufferings of his fellow man. The many friends of Melvin J. Maas will be appreciative of Mrs. Zehnpfennig's fine efforts.

—MIKE MANSFIELD,
Majority Leader,
United States Senate

Acknowledgments

If a man can be judged by the company he keeps, Major Gen. Melvin J. Maas led a life that was rich in congeniality. Never has a biographer enjoyed the encouragement of so charming and enthusiastic a "cheering section." Behind it is the inspiration of a man who rests on Pershing Hill—but who is still a lively, dearly beloved figure in the lives of those who knew him.

Starting at the top, there is a grand heritage of laughter in the Maas family. Frank N. Maas, Commander USNR (Ret.), was not only a gold mine of information, but he also kept me chuckling.

The members of the Maas family in the Washington area entertained me more as a friend than as a researcher. It was a thrill to meet the three Maas daughters, and Joe and his wife Connie, and Connie's parents, and Lee Catterton. There will be many "auld lang syne" hours to remember, with conversations that sparkled with anecdotes. This section would become another book if I tried to mention all of them. Let me only say that this is a very charming and attractive family. I am also most grateful to Mrs. Katherine Maas who was with us "in spirit" from her new home in Mexico.

My affection extends to the third generation—to a little doll named Christine Maas, and the winsome little Catterton girls. Needless to say, Marty Martino is an extremely special young man in my book. I will continue to be interested in the future activities of all of General Maas' grandchildren, including Kathy, Patti, Judi and Robbie Martino.

The files that Marianne Maas Catterton loaned to me provided much helpful information. "Mike" is the custodian of her father's diaries, his notes for "Soup With a Fork," and other papers which could become another book some day.

So many distinguished people were willing to pause in their busy lives to talk about General Maas. I thank Senator Mike Mansfield for his gracious co-operation, and Teddy Roe for his kind offer of assistance. The contribution from Speaker of the House John W. McCormack was received with gratitude.

It is difficult to express the warmth of my appreciation to Joe Bartlett and Charlie Jordan and all the colleagues and friends who knew Congressman Mel Maas on Capitol Hill.

After several days of "researching" General Maas at Marine Headquarters in Arlington, Virginia, I felt almost like a member of the Corps. Commandant Wallace M. Greene Jr., is not only a great officer—he also talks to women as though they are capable of comprehension. My brief conversation with

Lieut. Gen. Richard C. Mangrum was also valuable and enlightening. The Marine Corps is in excellent hands.

I am grateful to Lieut. Col. Patricia Maas for "opening the doors" to Marine Headquarters for me, and to the Marine Library personnel who cooperated in my research of the military records of General Maas, and to all the attractive, alert officers and enlisted Marines who were helpful to me at Headquarters.

With a son in MACS-7 at Chu Lai, my interest in the Marine Corps is not entirely impersonal. Sergeant Gary Zehnpfennig has helped me to avoid some rhetorical "pungi sticks," and his notes from Okinawa have vividly bridged the years between two generations of Marines. Thank you, Sergeant!

One of my first published sources of information was Colonel Tom Wert's "A Brief History of the Marine Corps Reserve Officers Association." This year, on the Fiftieth Anniversary of MCROA, the first full-length history of "The Marine Corps Reserve, 1916-1966," was compiled under the direction of Colonel William P. McCahill. A hardcover volume, it is sold by the Superintendent of Documents, U. S. Government Printing Office, Washington, D. C. Many fascinating details of Marine Corps history, including the famous mid-century "fight for survival" will be found in Colonel McCahill's book. Without the generous assistance of Marines who are also gifted historians, there would have been many gaps in this biography. A brisk salute to Colonel McCahill and Colonel Wert!

Speaking of Marine Corps colonels, I would like to thank Todd Hays and Daniel Omer—whom I almost didn't happen to meet. Both Colonel Hays and Colonel Omer contributed some splendid comments about General Maas.

My thanks to "Leatherneck" Magazine for printing a request for material about General Maas, and for much additional assistance. The letters from Mrs. Lynch Steiner of Glendale, Missouri, and Colonel W. McCombs of Washington, D. C., were especially helpful.

The hours I spent with members of the President's Committee on Employment of the Handicapped will always be dear to my heart. It was a great sensation to meet Harold Russell—in person! The President's Committee will keep surging ahead under his buoyant chairmanship. The Executive Secretary, Colonel Bill McCahill of the Marine Corps Reserve, likes to joke about the fact that he has a former Army sergeant—Harold Russell—for a boss. The versatility of Colonel McCahill has been noted throughout this book; it is evident that he can adjust himself cheerfully to almost any situation.

I should write a page of thank-you's to each of the delightfully obliging people in the President's Committee offices—Bernie Posner, the deputy executive secretary; Larry Burdick, the editor of "Performance;" Jimmy Jewett, the motion picture expert, and others whom I have met more briefly. I have enjoyed chatting with Dorothy Dunnigan, Rosemary Hunt, Leah Smuckler and Mrs. Taylor. The human race can learn a great deal that is worthwhile from the people up there on the seventh floor of the Department of Labor. They know that theirs is a special "labor of love," and it is reflected in their personalities.

My good IPA friend, Major Gen. Jim Dan Hill, U. S. Army (Ret.), was one of General Maas' colleagues. I thank General Hill for his reminiscences and for "clarifying some issues" for me.

It was a happy coincidence that Mr. Lawrence M. Brings, my publisher, attended Central High in St. Paul with Mel Maas and was able to observe him in action as a "young politician." Thank to Mr. Brings, there were some vivid recollections about that 1915 mock political convention.

Dr. and Mrs. J. Marion Bankhead are the present owners of the lovely home on Dale Drive. We are all most grateful to Mrs. Bankhead for the evening when she welcomed us so graciously and helped to bring a wealth of memories to life.

Whenever I spoke to anyone who knew Mel Maas, it was suggested that I also talk to several other people. At that rate, it might have taken twenty years to write this book. It is with mixed emotions that I also thank all the people with whom I did not talk.

I am indebted to Arlene Francis for the "Home Show" material, to the "Town Meeting of the Air" for excerpts from one of General Maas' speeches, to the "Georgetown Forum," and to a number of other excellent radio, TV, and motion picture productions.

I send greetings and salutations to all the fine people in the Melvin J. Maas Chapter of the Disabled

American Veterans in Suitland, Maryland. It was a pleasure to be with you in April.

As is customary with researchers, I deeply appreciate the cooperation of the two special libraries in my life—the Handley Library in Winchester, Virginia, and the Library of Congress in Washington. The Study Room Staff at the Library of Congress Annex could not have been more gracious and accommodating — they gave me a perfect place to pound my typewriter for several weeks. Most of this book was "original research" of the type that required intense concentration in huge volumes of the Congressional Record and similar government publications.

To all the people I have quoted briefly and at length, good health, good humor, and all the other blessings that Mel Maas would wish for you. You are marching in cadence—in his gallant company!

G. Z.

Chapter One

A Life Worth Living

History sometimes bequeaths to the world an individual who is always "on active duty"—a lovable human dynamo who is capable of living at least three distinct "lives" and surpassing all the normal requirements in each one.

This is the dramatic story of a Marine flyer who went from Curtis Jennys to jets, from Congress to Guadalcanal and Okinawa, from the drafting of armed forces-reserve legislation to a decade of spectacular service to humanity as Chairman of the President's Committee on Employment of the Handicapped. His gallantry in peace and war, his sense of humor and his devotion to human justice inspired President Lyndon B. Johnson to say of him: "He has shown us how to live in the face of adversity. His courage and conviction have enriched us all."

Melvin Joseph Maas was born in Duluth, Minnesota, on May 14, two springtimes before the turn of the century. Even in the spring, up in Paul Bunyan country, there may still be some obstinate snowflakes freshening the air and later-winter winds whipping gales across Lake Superior. It is a fine region for starting a stouthearted life.

Before young Mel was old enough to appreciate the breathtaking Duluth scenery, the Maas family moved farther south to Minneapolis for a short time and then put down roots in St. Paul, the Twin City on the other side of the Mississippi. There the father founded a bakery-supply firm.

The Maas parents took pride in their Irish-German-Dutch heritage, and they found plenty of kindred souls like themselves in St. Paul. Frank N. Maas, the father, was primarily of German descent. The mother's ancestors were mainly Irish. And with a name like Brady, what else would they be?

Mel and his brothers were reared on fabulous stories about their Irish grandfather, and his father before him, who sometimes uttered the proud boast that they were "run out of Ireland for teaching sedition against England." There are almost legendary tales about Grandfather Thomas Brady—a dashing young "Sinn Feiner" type, who came sailing over from Ireland about 1850, at the age of eighteen. He was not only cocky and handsome and bursting with the luck o' the Irish, but they say he was also expected. His ship was met at the pier by a delegation from Tammany Hall, and he was passed along to be educated by Irish-Americans who did well by him—and he by them.

Grandfather Thomas M. Brady lived with the family in his old age. Behind him was a gallant record as a Captain in the Union Army, where he had fought with special distinction at the Battle of Shiloh. He had become a judge and a very prominent citizen, with the biographical facts of his life being written up in "Who's Who in America." Mel's imagination was fired by this grandfather who came to seek his independence in the United States—but who could still be indignant about the shackles that bound his native County Claire and all the rest of Ireland. There will always be a warmth of feeling about Judge Thomas M. Brady in the Maas family. Even unto the third and fourth generations today, his descendants speak of him with a fine blend of rapture and respect.

The Maas household in St. Paul was an unusual one. As the oldest son, Frank, so aptly put it, "There were six of us boys and no girls to soften and dignify the family." He remembers Mel as a better than average student in school. From his earliest childhood the boy showed a demanding curiosity, wanting to know the reasons and causes for everything. The alert-minded youngster was not satisfied with easy answers that barely skimmed the surface.

Mel and T. Eugene, the "middle-aged" boys in the family, were close pals because they had much in common—including being caught in the middle. Frank and Clayton were the older brothers, and the two younger ones were named Kenneth and A. Bertram—but appropriate nicknames were applied to all of them.

It was a boisterous household, filled with high spirits and masculine humor. Mel was the sort of youngster who would roll on the floor, shaking with helpless laughter, when anything struck him funny. His appreciation for a good joke did not diminish through the years. As a grown man, he would sometimes laugh until the tears poured down his face.

The Maas boys attended Central High School in St. Paul. At Central, Mel may have propelled himself into a contest that shaped his future destiny. Lawrence Brings, who later became a Minneapolis publisher, has not forgotten the stimulating suspense of the mock political convention of 1915 in which almost two thousand students participated during a day-long and evening program patterned after the procedures followed at a regular political convention. He noted that it was more than just a one-day extravaganza. "For several weeks prior to the actual date of the convention there was exciting organization of the students into different political parties with the usual campaigning and maneuvering." As Mr. Brings recalls it, "There were about seven groups who were campaigning for their favorite candidates."

He remembers Mel Maas most vividly as a small young man, but a vigorous and persuasive one, who leaped into the political fray with fireball enthusiasm and revealed his natural talents as an organizer and as a spokesman for important issues.

Lawrence Brings, Mel Maas and Donald Countryman were the three ringleaders who manipulated a dark horse party into prominence. Young Brings was chosen to nominate their candidate, Charles Evans Hughes, who actually did run against Woodrow Wilson in 1915 and later became Chief Justice of the United States—but not President. If the trio of Brings-Maas-Countryman had managed Mr. Hughes' campaign, he might have reached the White House in 1916.

Brings nominated Mr. Hughes with an eloquent speech, and the three young politicians viewed the grand climax with jubilation. As a result of their political activity behind the scenes, Mr. Hughes was elected on the first ballot—against a large field of rival candidates. In looking back over the years to 1915, Lawrence Brings believes that Melvin Maas got his first taste of political activity during his high school days and that it whetted his appetite for future political achievement.

When his mother died that year, young Mel learned that sorrow can suddenly enter the life of a lusty, happy family. Because Frank Maas Sr. was in poor health at that time, the oldest son, Frank Jr., often acted as both father and mother to the houseful of younger brothers.

If all the Maas boys were as high-spirited as Mel, Frank must have had his hands full. "Mel loved motorcycles," Frank recalls, "and he was a fast rider who broke many a starting pedal. He wanted to race professionally, but we talked him out of that." All his life, one of Mel's legs would be marked with a scar he sustained when he scraped the road during a nasty accident.

Europe was already in a state of military chaos when Mel and his classmates were being graduated from Central High. The pros and cons of that mighty conflict had been debated during the mock political convention, but it still seemed quite remote. There was a formidable ocean stretching between the United States and the armies of "Kaiser Bill" in those days. Nobody was able to fly across casually in six or seven hours. It was scarcely a dozen years since Orville Wright had gotten his first crude "flying machine" off the ground for almost one whole minute at Kitty Hawk. When planes and flyers wanted to cross the Atlantic in 1916, they had to be transported in ships.

In February 1917, Germany announced that it would resort to unrestricted submarine warfare against all Atlantic shipping, including that of the neutral United States. President Wilson stopped trying to be a peacemaker between the belligerents and declared war on Germany in April.

On April 23, 1917, the military records show that a St. Thomas College student named Melvin Maas presented himself at the Marine Corps Recruiting office in St. Paul and expressed his determination to join up with the Leathernecks. With him was his best friend, Nathaniel Lufkin, who also wanted to enlist in the Corps.

A short time before, Mel had turned down an appointment to West Point. The peppery young fellow did not want to spend four years in a classroom while there was a war to be won. Why the Marine Corps? No one else in his family had been a Marine. Except for growing up near the Mississippi, Mel was a "landlubber." So were hundreds of other young men from Minnesota colleges who flocked to join the Marine Corps, mainly because they thought they could get into action sooner in a smaller outfit.

The Marines — the fabled "Leathernecks" — already had a history of going places fast. As the present Commandant, General Wallace M. Greene Jr., has pointed out, "The Marine Corps has traditionally provided our country with the ultimate in fighting men." This versatile "force in readiness" was created on November 10, 1775, by a resolution of the Continental Congress. In 1776, the Corps made a spectacular amphibious landing in the Bahamas and captured desperately needed powder and arms for George Washington's army.

Both the Navy and Marines were almost abolished for a period after the Revolutionary War, but later they were found to be downright indispensable. For much of the nineteenth century, the Marine Corps was one of the most important components of the naval service, serving with dauntless heroism in naval operations on the Barbary Coast, in the War of 1812, and in the Civil War. It has been the fate of the Marine Corps to be considered "unnecessary" at various peacetime periods, and that is what happened after the Civil War. Along came the Spanish-American War, and the value of a "military expeditionary force attached to the fleet" was again recognized as vitally essential, especially in the Philippines campaign.

Mel Maas liked the idea that the Marine Corps had already developed a reputation for "action with a special flair." Because he was still too young to enlist, Mel had to have his father's consent which was given with normal reluctance. Here was a teen-ager, wanting to set out for a faraway war. Both he and Nathaniel Lufkin were sent to Mare Island, California, where they enlisted officially "for the period of the war" and took their boot-camp training. There are some arguments about whether boot camp was more rugged in the days of the "Old Breed" than it is today, but the letters to parents of Marine recruits still state frankly: "The training program will demand his utmost effort, both physically and mentally . . . I am confident that . . . we shall be able to send back to you a fine Marine, a man grown stronger physically, morally and spiritually."

In his first photograph, Mel was pictured in the 1917 regulation uniform with a high, tight collar. His face, young and round, was topped by a head of curly black hair—to make a fine Irish combination with his blue eyes. He stood solid and erect in his boot camp boots with the regulation leggings buckled around them. That day he could say, "I am a Marine!"

When Private Maas learned that Marine Aero Company No. One was being formed in Cape May, New Jersey, his bouncing imagination soared skyward. That was what he wanted to be—an aviator!

Mel had learned to take emergencies in his stride at boot camp. When the troop train was wrecked on the way to Quantico, Virginia, he extricated himself from the overturned car and then made himself useful. Because he was small enough to squeeze in and out of tight places, the plucky young man assisted in the rescue of many troop passengers.

By July 14, he was with the 79th Company at Quantico, where he won his Marksman Medal. Before August was over, he was on active duty at Philadelphia with an outfit that bore the irresistible name of "Aviation Company."

In writing a full-scale biography about an almost legendary figure, it is sometimes necessary to separate "the man from the myth." Once in awhile someone says that Mel Maas went from Private to General in World War I. That would be a "neat trick" for a teen-ager, and it would undoubtedly discourage other ambitious young recruits. Maas did make Corporal in less than seven months, which was swift enough.

After several months with Marine Aero Company No. One at Cape May, New Jersey, the men returned to Philadelphia. If he had time to think, Corporal Maas must have figured he had done an amazing amount of training and traveling since he left St. Paul the previous April.

Early in January, the Aero Company men boarded the USS Hancock and set out on the wintry Atlantic for the Azores Islands, west of Portugal. All that time, Mel and Nathaniel Lufkin had managed to stay together—"buddies" in war as well as peace.

On that long boat trip, Mel could look up at the stars and imagine a time when men might hurl themselves on giant wings, even in the darkness of night, on "sky bridges" across the Atlantic. Night flying was still considered hazardous in 1918, and long-distance fuel problems had not begun to be solved.

Base Number 13 at Ponta Delgada on St. Miguel Island became "home" to the Marines of Aero Company Number One. At last Mel Maas was involved in the most thrilling assignment of his young life—scouting by air for German submarines and other enemy craft off the coast of Portugal. The young Minnesotan reveled in the excitement and challenge of being airborne. The planes they flew were the old Curtis Jennys, open to the elements and without any cozy modern refinements. During "dog fights," fire power was furnished by machine guns clamped to the fuselage, right in front of the cockpit. This was the first war in which the Marines were active in the air as well as on land and sea.

Marines are required to be versatile. Mel Maas also served sea duty, in charge of a Marine Detachment on board the USS New Hampshire. As a corporal and an acting sergeant with responsibilities for his men, the young noncommissioned officer wrote this list of enlightened suggestions "For Officers to Remember":

1. Talk to enlisted men in an official way only about necessary things, not things that are of no concern to officers; do not nag men and tell them to do things that they are about to do anyway or are doing; IN OTHER WORDS, DON'T INSULT THEIR INTELLIGENCE.

2. Give the men as much liberty as possible, consistent with good soldiering.

3. Leave a rest period between calls.

4. Set a good example to the men in everything, especially work.

5. Have the men always feel that they can come to you with real grievances, or for assistance, BUT do not gush with them or encourage undue familiarity.

6. Try to make the surroundings comfortable and as home-like as possible. Make things convenient. DON'T FORGET THAT THEY ARE MEN AND HUMAN.

7. After a bit of good work well done, don't begrudge A WORD OF APPRECIATION. IT IS ENCOURAGEMENT.

8. Inaugurate a system of both anonymous and credited suggestions, to be made at the liberty of the men.

9. Give the men as much liberty and leeway as possible and beyond that BE STRICT. Give them all you can give them, and THEN take NO kicking or grumbling.

10. To attain and keep harmony among the men, encourage getting together planned and extemporaneous shows with local talent. Provide plenty of means of recreation, reading and writing and music. DON'T MAKE THE AFFAIRS STIFF OR FORMAL OR EFFEMINATE. MAKE THE CAMP MORE ATTRACTIVE THAN TOWN.

Starting out as only a small, rejuvenated force in 1916, almost 73,400 United States Marines brought new renown to the Corps in "The Great War" during 1917 and 1918. The stubborn heroism of Leathernecks in the trenches of Chateau-Thierry and in Belleau Wood became a battlefront legend.

For more than two decades, textbooks and reference books would refer to the gigantic conflict of 1914-1918 as "The World War" and "The Great War." One war of that size, with its millions of casualties, seemed enough for modern civilization to bear.

On October 18, 1918, a young noncommissioned officer named Melvin Maas arrived back at Norfolk, Virginia. He had been appointed to take Officers' Training at Quantico, but the influenza epidemic was raging across the country. A flu germ did what the war had not been able to do—it laid Mel Maas low, very low.

Perhaps the doctors considered his prospects for survival hopeless, or else there was an appalling error in the records. Frank Maas Sr. in St. Paul was notified that his son was dead, and he made the long, sorrowful journey to bring him home. When he arrived in Norfolk, the elder Maas found that Mel was still weak but very much alive. It was a poignant reunion.

On November 11, the Armistice was signed, and the war was over for Mel and millions of other young men who had lived a "lifetime" during those months —on ships in submarine-infested waters, in trenches under shellfire, and in flimsy aircraft over land and sea.

Mel Maas packed up his duffle bag and went back home to St. Paul. Fully recovered, he was just as cocky as ever, with the same Irish twinkle in his eyes. He didn't know what the future held for him, but subsequent events proved that he was ready for almost anything.

On his military record, he was listed as "Excellent" in everything—Military Efficiency, Obedience, Sobriety, and Character in General. On July 30, 1920, he received the Good Conduct Medal for all the sterling qualities he had displayed during his term of enlistment in "The Great War."

Chapter Two

Politician and Pilot

Mel Maas took up his life again, but behind him would always be the remembrances of orderly discipline and good comradeship among his fellow Marines at Mare Island, Quantico, Philadelphia, Cape May, and especially Punta Delgada in the Azores. He had become quite a "world traveler."

After all that, it seemed as though his daily civilian routine might be humdrum for the young aviator, but he plunged back into campus life as a man of experience who had taken distant horizons in his stride. Given his choice of colleges, he chose to finish his education at the College of St. Thomas and the University of Minnesota. Debating continued to be his favorite extracurricular activity.

Nathaniel Lufkin proved to be a friend indeed. Mel had reached home first, after the war was over, and he felt it was fitting to keep his buddy posted on any news about his best girl friend, Katherine Bole —who was known to all her friends as "Jimby." Mel may have sounded overzealous, because Nathaniel wrote back, "Why don't you take Jimby out?"

Nathaniel must have been a mind reader. Mel began to date Jimby as soon as he had the "all clear" signal, and the romance led them to the altar.

Most of the Maas brothers were getting settled down by that time. Frank, the oldest one, has always been a fabulous person in his own right, with a sense of humor equal to Mel's. Among his recollections of their venerable grandsire, Thomas M. Brady, is this gem: "It had been my duty to take the Judge around on 'Decoration Day' to the schools where he would be decked out in full uniform and delighted the youngsters with his tales of the Civil War. He was very humorous, and he spoke seven languages, including profanity."

After Frank finished at St. Thomas College, he felt an urge to go into a promising new industry—the automobile business. Instead, he found himself trying to keep the family firm from going downhill. In the process of rejuvenating the Maas-Keefe Company—a bakery-supply concern—he "fell in love with it." Looking back over the years, Frank was glad his father had convinced him that the bakery-supply business could be just as fascinating and profitable as dealing in automobiles. Frank developed the firm to the point where it financed the educations of his brothers, and he in turn reared and educated a family of four.

While Frank was keeping the home fires burning, Clayt served as a Second Lieutenant in "The World

War." Gene received cadet training, but the war was over before he was old enough to serve. Both Kenneth and Bert were too young to think of military service.

The second brother, Clayton, tried the stationery business after the war and later became an excellent salesman and buyer in the Maas family firm. Gene went right into the Maas-Keefe Company and became one of the "finest salesmen in the business," according to Frank. After working for the Mars Candy Company in Virginia, Kenneth yearned for his Mississippi homeland. Both he and Bert later joined the family business in St. Paul.

Mel could have gone into the family firm, but his brother Frank recalls that the young bridegroom's mind was seething with ideas for inventions about that time. At the top of the list was a burglar alarm that was destined to make a life of crime extra hazardous—even for innocent bystanders. Mel had run into another imaginative soul who provided him with a "miracle chemical" which he put into thin glass bottles and sealed securely. These contraptions were suspended on thin wires inside of safes or any other place that might be robbed. The theory was that the bottles would break at the crucial moment and a strong tear gas would be released to overwhelm the intruder.

The amateur inventor was intensely serious about his burglar repellant, even though the rest of the world might have thought it funny. They laughed at Edison, didn't they? Mel was a great salesman. In spite of Frank's obvious skepticism, he talked his older brother into installing a few of the tear gas bottles at the Maas-Keefe Company. "But," Frank said, "when one of them got tired and broke by itself and drove the help out of the building, we threw them all out." (The "burglar bottles," not the help.) "By that time," Frank recalls, "all the others he had sold began to give trouble, so good honest Mel went around and gave the money back to each purchaser."

Mel experimented with other ingenious devices of his own invention, but it appeared that being a public speaker was his "real calling." He and Mrs. Maas left the tear gas and tinkering behind and led a jolly nomadic life for awhile. They got themselves a Model T Ford and toured the country, and Mel supported them with the fees he got for addressing various chambers of commerce and other civic and social groups. It was not as precarious as it sounds. Mel was a great talker, so they didn't miss any meals.

The lure of "black gold" in Texas slowed the ex-Marine down for a short spell, but he soon gave up trying to become a big oil man. He and Jimby headed back toward home country again.

In Omaha, Nebraska, Mel learned the fine arts of the insurance business, specializing in the selling of surety bonds. It was only a short hop back to St. Paul in 1924, and there Mel Maas seemed to have found his niche in life as a member of the Dwyer-Maas Insurance Agency which he established with his brother Gene and an associate named Tom Dwyer.

By 1926, Melvin and Katherine Maas had settled down among their relatives and old friends in a house on James Street in St. Paul. They were starting to rear a family of three vivacious little daughters. Mel was popular in his home city, and he was considered a highly competent young businessman.

If it hadn't been for a picture in the paper, Mel Maas might have gone on to become a leading insurance tycoon in the Twin Cities. A local cartoonist made a sketch of young Mr. Maas and commented that he thought Mel would make a "spiffy" looking Congressman.

Mel had actually grown up with a major campaign issue on his mind, but he hadn't intended to present it in person to his neighbors in the Fourth Congressional District of Minnesota.

But he had enjoyed all the political excitement of that mock election at Central, hadn't he? And he had lived dangerously, flying beyond the Azores in a flimsy plane to search for submarines, hadn't he? His eyes lighted up at the thought of sticking his head in the lions' den to argue the injustices of the Eighteenth Amendment.

St. Paul is the "nerve center" of the Fourth Congressional District of Minnesota. The second largest metropolis in Minnesota, it is also the state capital city. In the mid-1920's, St. Paul boasted a respectable number of handsome libraries, theaters and mansions. James J. Hill, of "Empire Builder" fame, was among the magnates who left their mark on the thriving pioneer city on the banks of the Mississippi. In spite of its cosmopolitan atmosphere, most of the voters in the Fourth Congressional District were considered loyal disciples of Andrew J. Volstead, the Minnesota Democrat who became renowned as "The Father of Prohibition."

Even in high school, Mel Maas had disputed the wisdom of prohibiting the sale of all liquor. The Eighteenth Amendment threatened to breed a new menace to society—gangsters who peddled illegal whisky and "bathtub gin," who terrorized cities by staging impromptu machine gun massacres, and fattened their pocketbooks on corruption. All the men in the Maas family had discussed the Eighteenth Amendment at length and had denounced it as much more of an evil than a blessing. They favored modification—light wines and beer—and they agreed to help Mel as much as possible if he would campaign primarily on that issue.

Including the father, there were seven of them when they were all at home. Mel weighed his prospects, catching the reflection of support and bravado in the eyes of his male kinfolk, and there was a look of resolution on his face as he nodded his curly head. Nothing ventured, nothing gained. This would be a crusade worthy of his irrepressible Irish temperament. He would fight the battle with logic and jaunty good humor, come what may. His older brother, Frank, recalls that period in his young brother's life with a warm surge of pride. He remembers that there was no stopping Mel when his enthusiasm began to boost him forward.

One of the local newspapers supported young Mel Maas. He was good copy, because there were very few politicians of any age who would dare challenge the awesome authority of Andrew J. Volstead, the sponsor of the leading Democratic candidate for Congress. This was no "pygmy" assignment that Maas had undertaken. Volstead had been a United States Congressman from 1903 through 1923; he would remain actively "dry" all of his life and be prepared to uphold those candidates who believed that the restrictions of the Eighteenth Amendment could make all Americans stop drinking.

Mel knew that Americans are likely to get very irked if someone tries to regulate them too much. Casual patronage of "bootleggers" and "speakeasies" had made a mockery of the high moral principles behind the Volstead Act. A majority of Americans abided by the law, but a powerful minority kept right on drinking.

Somehow Mel Maas, a political fledgling of twenty-six, awoke one morning to find that he—and his loaded-for-bear backers — had challenged the grand old patriarch of prohibition to a public debate. Before he could have his crack at the Volstead candidate in the primaries, Mel had to take on the giant himself. It was possible he would have welcomed the opportunity, election or no election, because he loved matching wits in a lusty argument.

Was the venerable Mr. Andrew Volstead shaking in his boots? In the jargon of his day, he promised to "cut that young whippersnapper down to size!"

Mel did not rush recklessly into a debate. He gathered his facts and figures with the cold, careful efficiency of a Marine leading an attack; he evaluated the strengths and weaknesses of his opponent's position, as well as his own. Beyond his boyish charm was a mind sharpened for combat.

Debates do not usually draw large audiences, but the St. Paul Auditorium was packed for the Volstead-Maas spectacular. For two decades, Andrew Volstead had been considered omnipotent, even by people whose party liquor was smuggled into the house underneath the laundry. He loomed high as a symbol of virtue, decency and clean American living.

The audience was convinced that no iconoclastic young puppy—Maas was only four years old when Volstead first went to Washington—would get anywhere. The "callow youth" surprised the audience. He ripped aside the curtain of respectability and revealed the demoralizing aspects of the Prohibition picture. It had given power and political influence to an underworld empire of thugs and criminals. One evil had taken the place of another. Too many police officers were being intimidated through threats or were blandly accepting "protection money." The American system of law and order was being threatened by the underworlds of New York and Chicago—and the Twin Cities would not be immune. It was fast becoming an unhealthy period in American history, with young people getting their "kicks" by carrying hip flasks to parties and drinking rot-gut liquor in murky hideaways known as "speakeasies."

Mel Maas emphasized that he did not favor strong intoxicants. He believed hard liquor would be less tempting if people were allowed to buy light wines and beer and drink them with legal dignity. Most Americans would be glad to stop doing business with gangsters, he reasoned.

Although the debate was not judged formally, Mel's dramatic plea for modification of the Eighteenth Amendment drew a mighty burst of applause from the audience. He made an impression that rippled to the far edges of Ramsey County and beyond. Whether he got anywhere or not, he knew he had dared to make people think.

Another young St. Paulite named Charles Jordan had become interested in Mel's activities. When he heard the debate at the auditorium, Charlie reacted with spirited enthusiasm. He immediately volunteered to be Mel's political organizer and campaign manager in the race for Congress.

They cleared the first hurdle when Mel survived as the Republican nominee in the primary. In the fall, he would be pitted against the strong Volstead Democrat, and Charlie recalls that the prospects looked poor. The high point had been that debate, and it sometimes seemed as though they had reached the climax too soon. The campaign continued to be a thrilling challenge for the exuberant amateurs, but they were stretching themselves almost too thin. There was no money in the campaign chest, the candidate looked too young, and a vote against the Volstead Act was almost a vote against religion.

The immediate Maas family and other kinfolk and friends set up a vigorous cheering section, but Charlie Jordan said that one key member experienced some qualms at a crucial moment. Frank Maas, Mel's father, called Charlie at one point and tried to talk him out of continuing the campaign—he thought it would be a waste of dedicated effort. But it was obvious to Charlie that Mel was making speeches in his sleep and was certainly not about to put the brakes on. Besides, if they stopped now, they would never know how it might have turned out.

Mel had another major plank in his platform as he rushed around the countryside delivering anti-Prohibition speeches. He favored adequate national defense in a world where humanity had not yet learned to live in peace and harmony. He would have been glad if the Great War had "made the world safe for democracy," but he was afraid the United States might be caught napping during some future military emergency. This was also a clear-cut issue because the Volstead faction favored disarmament.

In addition to the campaign furor that year, Mel Maas became a Marine again. Nothing in his life would be more significant. He had chosen that branch of the service in 1917 because it was considered an elite force—renowned through history for discipline, courage, and "esprit de corps." In 1926 he was invited to join the Marine Corps Reserve as an officer.

In "A Brief History of the Marine Corps Reserve Officers Association," Colonel Tom Wert noted that the Marine Reserve was composed of three officers and thirty-three enlisted men when the United States entered the World War in 1917. However, a high-spirited Massachusetts Naval Militia unit had formed a Marine Company and started drilling even before President Woodrow Wilson signed the first Marine Corps Reserve Act in 1916.

Most of the 73,400 Marines who fought in World War I were considered "reserves" who had enlisted for the duration. Some of them joined the regular Marine Corps after the Armistice, but most of them returned to civilian life as Mel Maas had done. Economic considerations and a feeling of security kept the armed forces at a minimum during the 1920's, but the Naval Reserve Act of 1925 authorized the creation of a Marine Corps Reserve and provided—quite frugally—for drill and annual training duty pay.

The Marine Reserve office at Headquarters in 1925 had a staff of only three officers and six clerks; but, according to "The Marine Corps Reserve, 1916-1966," ". . . this unit set the sights for a machine that was to proliferate and provide for thousands of men and women from the civilian population who would rally to the Corps and become indistinguishable within it as they fought for the common cause."

Would Mel Maas "rally to the Corps?" He argued both sides of the question in his mind. He loved the Marine Corps too much to consider giving the Reserves a niggardly amount of attention. He was extremely busy being a civilian, with his young family and the Congressional campaign and his insurance business. On the other hand, there would be an extra dimension to his life—with the opportunity to be both a civilian and a Marine again. When he heard that he would have a chance to fly again as a Marine aviator, that cinched it! On June 15, 1926, Melvin Joseph Maas was appointed a First Lieutenant in the Volunteer Marine Corps Reserve, and in August he flew with the Pilot Marine Corps Reserve at Quantico, Virginia, during a period of active duty.

During that year, Lieutenant Maas visited Washington and took a long, quizzical look at the Capitol as he was passing by. Would it have an important place in his life? He also went to see the Commandant of the Marine Corps to discuss a subject that had been simmering in his mind—the possibility of creating "a sizable, living, strong Marine Reserve force." The proposal received respectful consideration, both at Marine Headquarters and among the officers who were friends of the young lieutenant from Minnesota. That brilliant brainstorm was destined to produce one of the most prestigious military-civilian programs in the country today.

As a political campaigner, Mel was developing more momentum than ever, and perhaps he received a fresh transfusion of buoyancy whenever he took a plane soaring up into the sky. Charlie Jordan, earthbound, remembers the awful suspense of those months before the election and the superb eloquence of the young candidate as he presented himself before one audience after another. Could it all evaporate into nothing?

The votes were counted more slowly in those days, and Mel did not know until the morning after the election that the citizens of his district had actually chosen him to speak for them in the House of Representatives in Washington. He had worked so persistently for it, but it was unbelievable. The papers were calling him "the baby Congressman." Mel took a critical look in the mirror and started growing a mustache.

Just a few days after the election, on November 10, a group of bright young men who wanted to serve both as civilians and Marine officers gathered to discuss a subject of far-reaching consequences. First Lieutenant Melvin Maas and Captain Harvey L. Miller were part of the small contingent that formed the Marine Corps Reserve Officers Association on the 151st Birthday of the U. S. Marine Corps. Maas was elected president—an office that turned out to be almost alarmingly permanent—and Miller became secretary.

A statement of worthy objectives was drawn up at that time, and it was agreed that MCROA would strive "to voice its views on the creation of strong reserve forces before the Congress of the United States and in the halls of the Navy and War Departments and at the White House."

Chapter Three

Mr. Maas Goes To Washington

Mel Maas had always moved at a brisk pace, and he was prepared for even faster acceleration as Congressman-Lieutenant Maas. Charlie Jordan had become an indispensable political aide. When young Mr. Maas set out for Washington, Charlie became his righthand man and Congressional assistant. At first Charlie thought he could handle every bit of the complicated legislative business emanating from the office, but he later discovered that no one person could cope with the multiplicity of "Maas activities" —not even if he worked all night.

The Journal of the House of Representatives for the First Session of the 70th Congress—"held under the Constitution of the Government of the United States and in the one hundred and fifty-second year of the Independence of the United States"—lists ten Congressmen from Minnesota, with the name of Melvin J. Maas appearing for the first time.

During the years ahead, he would hammer hardest on the subjects of national defense legislation, unemployment, fiscal integrity, development of aeronautics—and the Volstead Act. He would also lend his support to dozens of other miscellaneous causes. Charlie Jordan remembers him as a "dynamic speaker" in Congress, throwing his entire weight behind each message because he believed in the rightness of his stand. He did not like to waste time on trivia. Refusing to serve the traditional period as "a timid freshman Congressman," he was inspired and stimulated to state his views from the first.

In 1927 he was appointed to serve on the Committee on Foreign Affairs, at a time when the United States did not have quite so many foreign affairs. It was obvious, however, that the blue-eyed Irishman from Minnesota was determined to protect the interests of his country. Among his fellow Committee Members were Hamilton Fish Jr. of New York, and "Joe" W. Martin of Massachusetts. Maas was most influential during that period in sponsoring the First International Congress on Sanitary Aviation and several other international conferences designed to promote better relations with foreign powers.

In a letter to Marine Corps Headquarters during his first year in Congress, Mel pointed out with a respectfully straight face that there was a slight discrepancy in his teen-age military record. "You have listed as overseas service my two trips in transit, to and from the Azore Islands, but have marked that time served in the Azores as home service . . ." They gave his letter as much prompt attention as though he had been a Colonel in "The Great War," instead of a "noncom." Mr. Maas' address, of course, was the United States House of Representatives.

The voters of the Fourth District in Minnesota liked the dash and verve of the new Republican Congressman so much that they sent him back for a second term. He was eager to return because he was desperately concerned about the continued reduction of defense appropriations. On every possible occasion, he had spoken on the need for keeping the military front strong and alert. The more indifference he encountered, the fiercer his anxiety became.

Right up to the eve of President Hoover's 1929 address to the joint session of Congress, Maas kept reminding his colleagues that the Chief Executive, the Cabinet, the two Houses of Congress and the members of the Supreme Court would all be assembled in the Capitol at one time. "If anyone dropped just one bomb from a plane, it would be the end of our national government. This country needs better protection," he insisted.

It sounded so farfetched that the complacent Congressmen thought they were hearing a fairy tale. Washington was not vulnerable. It couldn't happen here!

Such lighthearted apathy, Maas reasoned, called for a demonstration that it could happen here. Instead of strolling sedately into that joint session, he rushed out to Bolling Field and was soon circling Washington in a small World War I pursuit plane. Exactly at noon, when the statesmen and dignitaries of the nation had settled down to listen to the President's message, a thunderous roar shook the Capitol. Maas, who had learned the new technique of dive-bombing during the Great War, aimed the plane at the House skylight with careful calculation—and then zoomed out and away.

There was havoc in the House chamber. Some of the distinguished gentlemen jumped up and rushed into the corridors. Those who recalled Mel Maas' admonitions brushed flakes of plaster from their clothing, and realized with tardy apprehension that it could have been a bomb.

Charlie Jordan was in his office that day, right next to a window, and he said the racket was fearful. About the time the air cleared, the phone rang. It was the Commandant of the Marine Corps, sounding extremely agitated and demanding to speak to Mel as soon as he came in. Evidently the news had traveled as fast as that little pursuit plane.

The aeronautical ace of Capitol Hill was still full of beans and bravado when he strode into the office, but he said, "Oh, oh," when he heard he was supposed to call General Nevill immediately. Charlie could hear him saying in a slightly deflated voice, "Yes, sir. No, sir," and, "Maybe I shouldn't have done it." After some discussion, it was decided that the flying eagle of the Marine Corps Reserve needed to report for urgent duty outside the District of Columbia for awhile.

Mel had rushed away before Charlie got all the particulars, which was just as well from Charlie's point of view. He was able to plead ignorance when he got a frantic call from St. Paul, Minnesota. The New York Times had "scooped" Mel's hometown paper with the "buzzing" story. What did Charlie know about it? Charlie said he didn't know the details, and he couldn't get hold of Mel because he was on his way out of town. The frustrated reporter said he would call back in a couple of days, but Charlie continued to be vague about the whole business. He had decided it might be indiscreet, for political purposes, to let the voters back home know that Mel had pulled a stunt like that. They might leap to the conclusion that he was "reckless!"

Mel was not reluctant to discuss the joint session fiasco himself. "People said that no plane could get within ten miles of the Capitol. I wanted to show that one bomb could wipe out the entire Government," he told reporters later on, and his colleagues were more inclined to agree with him. At least they agreed that the blue yonder was a whole lot wilder when he was up there.

Congressman Maas might have been jeopardizing his future as a Captain in the Aviation Section of the Marine Corps Reserve when he used such a devastating type of "air mail" to deliver his own "message to Congress."

Mel had already been appointed a Captain in the Volunteer Marine Reserve, and he had flown with both the Regulars and the Reserves during training periods. In February 1929, he requested assignment to the Aviation Section of the USMCR, stating the following qualifications: "I hold a pilot's license from the Department of Commerce; served in the Marine

Corps aviation branch in 1917 and 1918, and have had considerable instruction in military aviation at the U. S. Army schools at Brooks and Kelly fields, San Antonio, Texas."

Under a letterhead reading, "Headquarters, U. S. Marine Corps Aviation Section," a memorandum for the Major General Commandant of the Reserve Section stated, on June 17, 1929: "Having satisfactorily completed an examination before a board of officers, appointed by the Major General Commandant, to examine Marine Corps Reserve Student aviators for designation as Naval Aviators, and in accordance with the approved recommendation of the board, it is requested that Captain Melvin J. Maas, USMCR, be designated a Naval Aviator, Marine Corps Reserve, as of June 12, 1929." The next month, Captain Maas was on active aviation duty and training for two weeks with Aircraft Squadrons, East Coast Expeditionary Force.

Mel was still a young man, scarcely thirty years old, and filled with appreciation and zest for life. It seemed incomprehensible that his lovely wife, his "Jimby," should be taken from him and their three little daughters when the future was opening before them.

There were the rosaries murmured with devotion, the flowers, the funeral mass—all the blessings of their church to dull the sharp edges of a young husband's grief. Frank Maas, the big brother who had often tried to be both a "mother and father" to Mel, remembers that it was a time of "terrible shock." But he also remembers that Mel threw himself back into all his activities and responsibilities—carrying on more energetically than ever, instead of brooding about his personal heartache.

Uppermost in his mind were the three winsome little girls who are still living proof that Katherine Bole Maas must have been a very attractive lady. The oldest child, Marianne, was nicknamed "Mike." It was poetic justice that the second girl was named Patricia to assure a proper "Pat and Mike" combination in the family.

Since it was obvious that no Congressman would have time to represent his constituents if he were trying to keep track of three little girls in Washington, Mel arranged for Pat and Mike to attend a boarding school in southern Minnesota. Grandfather Maas fretted about that arrangement, so they went to live at his house on Goodrich Avenue in St. Paul until the family was later reunited. It was a very large house on a corner lot, Pat recalls, and was dramatically decorated with a turret-shaped tier of bay windows three stories high.

The littlest tot was baptized Katherine, but she grew up answering to the name of "Sandy." Feeling adequate to cope with one small child, Congressman Maas took Sandy to Washington with him—to the sacred halls of Congress once in awhile, and more often to the Cannon House Office Building.

Once Sandy turned up missing from her father's office in the Cannon Building—here one minute, gone the next, in the mysterious manner of small children—and she recalls hearing that there was quite a commotion, with her father and other distinguished Congressmen and secretaries dashing frantically around the halls searching for a little lost girl. Finally they thought to look under the couch in her father's office—and there she was, fast asleep.

Congressman Maas continued to be a "fighting Irishman" on such diversified subjects as national defense, promotion of aviation, protection of American business, the Volstead Act, and the fiscal policies of the United States Government. He protested the selling, leasing or dismantling of various naval vessels used for training purposes, and he showed his concern for the people who had already served by calling for a 350-bed addition to the Veterans Hospital at Fort Snelling, near Minneapolis.

Early in 1931, Maas uncovered a post office scandal in his home city of St. Paul. His own party had netted more than a million dollars in "political patronage" contributions. Mel Maas threatened to stay out of the Republican caucus that year unless he received the right to supervise the post office on his own high level of integrity. He would always be the same "poor honest Mel" who had refunded all the money for those tear gas contraptions.

On Capitol Hill that year, the aviation-conscious Congressman from Minnesota made a speech that now has the ring of "ancient history." He urged more planes for South American service, pointing out that Pan American, the largest American company operating an international airline at that time, made only one air mail trip a week from Miami to Santos, Brazil.

Maas noted that European airlines were becoming brisk competitors in that potentially rich market—but "we had shown that we could get there faster," so we should be doing equally as much to stimulate "good will and cordial relations."

Charlie Jordan remembers the instant eloquence of Mel Maas. "He could sit down and dash off a speech in nothing flat."

When he talked informally, Mel's favorite topic also was flying. In the spring of 1930 he was commissioned a Major in the Marine Reserve and assigned to the Fleet Marine Corps Reserve. In June 1931, he was transferred to the Naval Reserve Air Base at Chamberlain Field near Minneapolis. During the three succeeding years, he reported to Quantico for two weeks of instruction every year, but most of his active duty time was spent at the Minneapolis field.

Actually, Mel flew wherever he possibly could, and that included the Washington area. At one facility, the Reserves could fly every Wednesday when the Regulars were off the field. Every Wednesday, Mel went dashing out to take up a plane.

Once he invited Charlie Jordan to go with him, and Charlie was disconcerted when the aviation officials asked some searching questions about his fitness to go aloft in one of those flying machines. What got him most "shook up," before he even got off the ground, was when they asked for the names of his next of kin. They must have seen he was going up with the dashing, daring aviator who had rattled the skylight on the Capitol.

That flight made a permanent impression on Charlie because Mel went hedge-hopping with glorious disregard for the law of gravity—zooming up and down like a roller coaster sometimes, about fifty feet above the ground. Charlie still gets a giddy look in his eye when he recalls the way they ruffled the treetops, and there is a lingering note of relief in his voice when he remembers how happy he was to get out of that plane when it landed. Other old friends recall similar experiences.

It could be assumed that Mel Maas flew with utter disregard for life, limb and aircraft, but he was often in the air and always seemed to have everything under control, week after week and year after year. To him, an airplane was more than a close friend—it was an extension of himself.

Integrity, loyalty and courage were Mel Maas' strongest traits. It mattered not that economy-minded President Hoover was the chief executive of his own party. When the President actually dared to mention the unmentionable—an outrageous plan to eliminate the Marine Corps by merging it with the Army—Congressman Maas got his Irish up and the sparks began to fly. In all fairness to President Hoover, the country was in the throes of the Great Depression, and he was seeking to reduce expenditures. But why, Mel Maas wanted to know, did he think he could save money by shoving the Marine Corps into the Army where the actual cost of training was higher?

Depression or no depression, the Congressman from Minnesota—who was also President of MCROA

—collected enough contributions from his fellow Reserve officers and other Marine Corps admirers to pay for speaking time on a nationwide radio hookup. There was no lack of eloquence as Maas entreated the people of the United States "not to permit the dissolution of this great Corps of elite fighting men." A deluge of telegrams persuaded President Hoover that the Corps must survive, but he made a futile attempt to reduce it to a minimum strength of ten thousand men.

When Mel Maas worried about the lack of defense preparedness, it was not a case of blind militarism. He had seen that "The Great War" had not made "the world safe for democracy" across the Atlantic. The tempers of some European powers were seething again, and Maas caught the danger signals and took them seriously.

Mel Maas was sending up plenty of signals of his own—smoke signals. The Congressman had a standing order for ten boxes of cigars a month, an excellent brand made in St. Paul and sent to him by way of New York. Shortly before each new batch was due on the first of the month, Mel would get restless and want to know, "Haven't my cigars come yet, Charlie?" One day Charlie Jordan did some mental arithmetic and asked, "Are you actually smoking five hundred cigars a month, Mel?" It was more of an exclamation than a question.

Chapter Four

Gunman in the Gallery

During that period of lengthy Congressional sessions, the statesmen of the nation were seeking to solve the problems of unemployment and economic stagnation that had gripped the country during the Depression.

When the House of Representatives convened on December 14, it appeared to be a normal day of activity. Unlike the Senate, which is famous for its air of semideserted dignity, the bustling House chamber often seems crowded with members. Eager speakers follow one another in rapid succession, as though aware that their two-year terms are fleeting fast.

On the afternoon of the 14th, a vote was being taken on a treasury bill amendment. Suddenly interrupting the teller's crisp roll call and the answering "yeas" and "nays," the relative tranquility of the lofty chamber was shattered by a challenge from the visitors' gallery, above and to the rear.

Visitors to the galleries of Congress are scarcely to be seen and certainly not to be heard, but this voice demanded in no uncertain terms, "I want twenty minutes to address the House."

Representative Edith Nourse Rogers of Massachusetts, who was seated directly below the gallery, looked up and screamed, "He's got a gun!"

"It's a bomb!" someone else cried.

Representative McMillan of South Carolina was seated in the Speaker's chair, facing the gallery. He took one look upward, rose slowly to his feet and stood transfixed during the grim battle of wits between a Congressman who never forgot he was a Marine, and a demented gunman who wanted attention at any price.

Most of the members of the House, seated facing the Speaker's dais, looked over their shoulders and prudently realized that this might be "the voice of doom." There was a moment of paralysis, and then a headlong exodus from the chamber was accelerated by a woman's shrill shriek from the gallery. The evacuation was not orderly. "Members tumbled over each other, some falling flat in the pell-mell scramble for exits," newsmen wrote afterward. The newsmen themselves dispersed hurriedly and peeped at the drama through cracks in the hallway doors.

To the left of the Speaker's dais, up in the front row of the gallery, stood the cause of the commotion—the stranger who kept waving his gun menacingly at his escaping audience.

One member stood alone among the empty seats, poised to meet the moment of desperation with calculated composure. Representative Maas strolled slowly toward the balcony, his eyes fixed on the face of the man above him. The unwelcome visitor had one leg over the rail as though poised to leap. Maas said afterward that he thought the man might leap or fall, and then it would have been easy to subdue him. But the man did not fall, and now he concentrated all of his antagonistic attention on the lone figure beneath him. For a moment, this one person symbolized all of Congress to him.

He heard Maas say in a firm, calm voice, "Come on, buddy, toss me the gun."

"I want to be heard. I demand my right of free speech."

"All right, son," Mel Maas told him softly. "I'll give you twenty minutes. But we have rules here. You can't speak with a gun. Come on, give me the gun."

There was a glassy look in the young man's eyes as he aimed the barrel at Maas and shouted, "I'll give it to you."

Around him, spectators in the gallery sat frozen with horror, waiting for the crack of the pistol.

Instead, there was a glint of blue steel as the man slowly turned the weapon until he held it by the barrel and then dropped it straight down. Maas' hand darted out expertly and caught the gun at the grip. The Congressman examined the weapon. It was a .38-caliber revolver, loaded in every chamber and cocked to fire. After releasing the hammer and placing it at safety, Maas strode to the Speaker's desk with considerable aplomb and laid down the revolver.

At that moment there was a flurry of activity in the gallery. Another House member had been carrying out a rear-guard action. Representative Fiorella La Guardia, who later became even more renowned as a great mayor of New York City, had dashed up to the gallery and was ready to seize the deranged intruder just as the gun was dropped down to Maas. He and several security men overpowered the befuddled gunman and led him away.

Representative La Guardia, it was noted at that time, was also an aviator who had a distinguished war record.

There were sighs of relief in the gallery from visitors who had sat frozen in their seats during those tense minutes. One man said he had tried to reason with the gunman, but had decided that silence was the best policy when he found himself staring into the barrel of the revolver.

It was typical of Mel Maas to want to speak with the man who had caused the greatest commotion in the House in fifty years. He could have dismissed the culprit as a "maniacal crackpot," but he wanted to know if he had an honest grievance. Those were the years of the Depression when insecurity and hopelessness sometimes drove men to suicide and other violent acts.

In the Senate guardroom, Congressman Maas learned that the man he had disarmed was a department store clerk named Marlin Kemmerer, from

Allentown, Pennsylvania. He also learned that he had been staring death starkly in the face during those moments of suspense. If Kemmerer had pulled that trigger, he would not have missed. "I have had the revolver for a long time," he told Maas. "I use it every day for target practice. I know how to shoot."

An icy chill caught up with Mel Maas at those words. "It felt good to have a whole skin," he said later. "At the time I didn't think so much about that. It was clear that the gun had to be taken away. I was afraid he might get excited and kill somebody. So, I just walked across the floor, talking to him in a friendly way, but as earnestly as I could."

It was difficult to know what Kemmerer had expected to accomplish with his desperate plea for attention. He said he wanted to inform the House about "terrible conditions in the country and to urge correction." He even had a typewritten petition in his pocket, ready to read to the House—with a gun in his hand to make the lawmakers listen.

Maas seemed almost surprised to receive a rousing ovation from his admiring colleagues outside the House chamber. Newsmen and photographers hung on his words and maneuvered for pictures.

An Illinois legislator, after praising Congressman Maas, made a joking reference to his gangster-ridden home city. "I think I'll go back to Chicago where I'll be safe from gunplay," he said.

Kemmerer, who maintained he was "for all the people," was held by the police for mental observation. They investigated rumors of grudges against several officials that might have set him to brooding about personal "injustices." Most of his story sounded as irrational as his actions had been. When two sticks of dynamite were found in his rented room in Washington, Kemmerer told police he had originally intended to blow himself up after he delivered his speech to Congress. He calmly confided that he had decided to use the revolver instead, so he would not injure anyone else.

The nation's papers, that night and the next morning, lauded the thirty-three-year-old Congressman from Minnesota who had looked death in the face and had spoken in cool, conciliatory tones to an armed gunman. He had even called him "son."

That same evening, front page headlines in the "St. Paul Pioneer Press" proudly proclaimed: "MAAS DISARMS GUNMAN MENACING HOUSE AS SOLONS FLEE FROM ROOM IN PANIC." In an enthusiastic account of the episode, reporter Alfred D. Stedman saluted the cool-witted courage of the Minnesota Congressman who was being "hailed as a hero by his colleagues." A picture of the intrepid Mr. Maas, complete with a fine head of black hair and a debonair mustache, accompanied the story. He looked out at his "public" with the usual Irish twinkle in his eyes.

Reporter Stedman noted that Representative Maas was the only licensed aviator in Congress at that time and that he had long been known as the "flying Congressman." It was an appropriate moment to recall the service record of a man who had not paused to wonder if he would rather be a sensible survivor than a dead hero: "A Major in the Marine Corps Reserve and commander of a Marine combat squadron, Maas served in the AEF during the World War, hunting by plane for submarines off the coast of Portugal."

It might have been said that Congressman Maas went out "in a blaze of glory." On the other hand, it seemed as though the Twentieth Amendment—changing the date for the convening of the Federal Government—was passed just late enough for him to be present for an historic occasion. He had already been "adjourned temporarily" from office on the sweeping tide of President Franklin D. Roosevelt's landslide victory, but 1933 was still the year when the incumbent Administration and Congress stayed in office until March.

Long before he had been elected to office, Mel Maas had started denouncing Prohibition. In Congress, he kept pointing out that it was a national farce—and a dangerous one. Gangsters were living like lords on illegal liquor profits. They were building up huge, flexible organizations to perpetuate their empires of vice through other criminal operations in the decades far ahead.

Congressman Maas could talk endlessly about thousands of deaths from alcohol which the government had purposely denatured and the bootleggers had imperfectly "purified" and sold to thirsty customers. He had told the House, in July 1932, that each state should be allowed to handle its own liquor legislation and enforcement ". . . in the interests of the health and morals of its citizens, to eliminate the public corruption and dangers inherent in Federal prohibition." He believed that "the powers conferred by the Federal government by the Eighteenth Amendment are police powers."

He had harped so energetically about the scandals of the Eighteenth Amendment that people kept asking, "Well, why don't you stop talking and do something about it? We're getting tired of listening to that story!"

The issue of repeal was one of the strongest planks in the Democratic platform in 1932, and many of the Republicans felt the same way. On February 20, 1933, the House joined the Senate in voting overwhelmingly in favor of the Twenty-first Amendment which finally repealed the Eighteenth—after ratification by three fourths of the states.

It might be assumed that Congressman Maas boomed out a resounding "Yea" and perhaps took a bow on that fateful February 20. He wasn't even there! Charlie Jordan remembers with a chuckle that the frustrated anti-Volstead crusader was stranded in Chicago by a blizzard. As far as that vote was concerned, he was just as "dry" as Andrew Volstead—and he certainly took plenty of kidding about it. "He never heard the end of that!" Charlie said.

Chapter Five

A Strong Defense

In 1933 Mel Maas returned to a second successful career in the insurance business in St. Paul. The peppery legislator from Minnesota may have been gone from Congress, but he was not forgotten. His "skywise" spirit had made an impact on some aviation-minded men.

As usual, the full tide of popular opinion had not yet caught up with Maas. According to these excerpts from an editorial in the St. Paul Pioneer Press for December 13, 1932, airplanes had no business trying to fly the Atlantic: ". . . There will doubtless be general agreement with the recently delivered opinion of the National Advisory Committee for Aeronautics that science has so far failed to develop a heavier-than-air plane capable of efficient transoceanic air transport service to Europe." It was concluded "that for the present, dirigibles are best for ocean use. Even if heavier-than-air planes increase in performance, reliability and speed, opinion will doubtless prevail that lighter-than-air craft are better adapted for transatlantic travel."

In Mel's mind, dirigibles were already past history. Airplanes were on the verge of commanding the skies—a fact he was trying to prove when he "buzzed" the Capitol. With an imagination alert to all the possibilities and probabilities, he worried about the vulnerability of his country in a period before the introduction of such modern safeguards as the Strategic Air Command, sophisticated radar equipment, and underground missile installations.

Major Mel Maas continued to fly with the Reserves — as exuberantly as a bird with unclipped wings, loving the disciplined freedom of climbing and maneuvering high above the earth. He could hardly wait until the aircraft industry got out of diapers and realized its mature potential.

Maas' aeronautical ambitions did not always suit the temper of those depression years. In 1931, the Marine Reserves were cut off without drill pay or funds for uniforms. With typical Marine resourcefulness, they outfitted themselves and continued to drill without pay. Major Maas not only trained at Quantico without pay, but he organized the first Marine Aviation Squadron at the Naval Air Base at Chamberlain Field in Minneapolis on a nonpay basis. Fortunately the Navy supplied aircraft for the weekly drills.

The Marine Reserves—on land and sea and in the air—might have dwindled away to nothing during those frustrating years, but Marines have a unique reputation for persevering against unbelievable odds. They cuss bitterly and grit their teeth and laugh—and keep going. One of their great inspirations during those lean years was Major Maas. As national president of the Marine Corps Reserve Officers' Association and a Marine Aviation Squadron leader, he kept the "esprit de corps" banner flying high from coast to coast.

Although he was not a member of Congress in 1933 and 1934, his courageous disarming of the gunman in the balcony of the House was still remembered with respect. On April 28, 1933, the Carnegie Hero Fund Commission announced the award of a silver medal to former Congressman Maas for saving "indeterminate person or persons from homicidal attack . . ."

Many decades later, one of Mel Maas' colleagues would describe him as both a farsighted Congressman and an outstanding Marine. It was said of him, "For more than a quarter of a century, he advocated a strong national defense and a trained, ready reserve to preserve international peace."

In recognition of his ability as a statesman, Mel Maas was returned to Congress in the 1934 elections. That campaign was enlivened by an extracurricular development. During one of the political rallies, some friends introduced Mel to an attractive young lady named Katherine Endress.

A widower with three small daughters, Mel had not forgotten his first Katherine, and he had not considered marrying again. He had been too busy even to think about it. Suddenly he became very much preoccupied with the idea.

Mel always had a boyish flair for flamboyant gestures. Miss Endress was in the party of friends who attended the State Fair in St. Paul that year, and Mel strained himself to impress her by driving a car in the stock car races. It was a sizzling performance. As it turned out, Miss Endress did not care much about races, but she did care about Melvin Maas.

Congressman Maas won both a bride and the election that year. The family became complete, with two parents for the little girls again. The girls grew up loving Katherine Endress Maas and calling her "Mother."

During their young years in Washington, the little Maas girls became fond of the Cannon Building —which was then known as the Old House Office Building. Sandy felt particularly lucky to need treatment from a dentist in that neighborhood, so she could drop in on her father more often. At that age, she wasn't too impressed by the celebrities she encountered. Her father, she believed, was the most important man in the world.

On one occasion, Congressman Maas and little Sandy were invited to have lunch with no less a personage than Sam Rayburn, the Speaker of the House. Mel Maas thought it was an event that should be engraved forever upon his daughter's impressionable young memory. At dinner with the family that night, he turned to Sandy and said, "Tell everybody the name of the gentleman we ate lunch with today." And he waited expectantly, looking pleased.

"I don't know," Sandy answered after a long

pause. She could only remember that the great Mr. Sam was "a nice man."

Names meant a great deal to Mel Maas. During his public life, it is estimated that he knew the names of four or five thousand people. First names were more important to him than last names, and he felt that it was just as important to know the name of a waiter or janitor as the name of a General. Under the circumstances, he sometimes ran into a bit of "memory trouble" himself, and it bothered him terribly. Sandy recalls that he told her she should walk on—as though she didn't know him—if he didn't immediately call her over to meet someone he encountered in the corridors of Capitol Hill. Almost everyone was a friend, but occasionally it was difficult to match all the names with the faces.

Back in Congress in 1934, Mel Maas was in his dynamic glory as the newest member of the House Naval Affairs Committee, under the chairmanship of Congressman Carl Vinson of Georgia. Charlie Jordan officiated as Maas' Congressional secretary again, and his eyes still glow with astonishment as he recalls the achievements of the Vinson-Maas team at a critical period in world history. Between the two of them, Vinson and Maas brought a "spectacular" number of bills to the floor and got practically all of them passed in the next several years.

History had gone full circle since "The Great War," and several nations again considered military aggression almost fashionable. Once more the complicated intrigues of "international power politics" were being viewed as inevitable. Strong nations felt justified in going to war to get what they coveted, and weak nations had no defense except their protective alliances with more formidable powers. Mel Maas, with an eye cocked toward restless Europe, could see that some old antagonists were "choosing up sides" again. The rhythm of the Nazi tide, goose-stepping into the pages of modern history, sounded more ominous to him than to most Americans.

Out in the Pacific, the Japanese were already plotting a "Japanese Co-Prosperity Sphere" designed to conquer and dominate much of China and Southeast Asia. The future appeared disastrous for the dove of peace. After the scuttling of the League of Nations, war was again being accepted as the ultimate solution to the world's problems.

Would the United States become involved again? Congressman Maas, studying the "chips on the shoulders" of various belligerent nations, was convinced that the Ship of State should be kept seaworthy.

President Franklin D. Roosevelt believed that reliance on aircraft carriers would be merely a temporary tactic. Congressman Maas, a man who had grown up with Marine pilots, disagreed vehemently and at length. The fiery Irishman, speaking his mind in the House of Representatives, demanded and got bigger and better aircraft carriers. Warships—most of them now in moth balls—advanced from fifty to eighty tons to match the hulking sea giants of other major nations. Many of the huge "flat tops" and warships that would see action during the decades ahead were built because a man from landlocked Minnesota believed they were necessary. "A lot of those big ships patrolling the oceans can be traced back to Mel Maas," Charlie Jordan said with quiet pride.

Early in his ten years of vociferous activity on the House Naval Affairs Committee, Maas not only introduced legislation for larger and better ships, but he often advocated a two-ocean Navy—as though he could glimpse a future threat on both horizons. Congressman Maas was as much of an asset to the Navy as to the Marine Corps.

In his other field of operation, Major Maas' devotion to active duty with the Marine Corps Reserve merited him another promotion. In 1935, when he was scarcely thirty-six years old, he was appointed a Lieutenant Colonel in the Marine Reserve.

The Marine Reserve units had sought valiantly to survive on meager appropriations. It was more than a coincidence that their plight was brought to the attention of the House Naval Affairs Committee in 1935. Congressman Maas was a firmly established member of the committee by that time.

In his "Brief History of MCROA," Colonel Tom Wert noted the solid accomplishments of the committee in its recommendations for a strong Marine Reserve force. The proposed Drilling Reserve would total 485 officers and 6,500 enlisted men (including 210 officers and 1,000 enlisted personnel in the aviation wing). The authorized strength of the Volunteer Reserve would be 2,155 officers and 16,050 enlisted men (including aviation).

Colonel Wert notes that Mel Maas was making

history for the Marine Corps Reserve: "In 1936, Congressman Maas, as a senior Republican member of the House Naval Affairs Committee, introduced a bill in the House of Representatives which called for a complete and comprehensive reorganization of the Naval Reserve bill. This bill ultimately became the Naval Reserve Act of 1938, which in turn became the cornerstone of the Naval and Marine Corps program as we know it today."

Ahead lay an authorized Marine Reserve program with provisions for an equable promotion system, increased drill pay, uniform gratuities, and even retirement disability benefits. There was also a hint of prestige in the establishment of Naval and Marine Corps Reserve Policy Boards appointed by, and reporting directly to, the Secretary of the Navy.

During the drafting of the Act, Congressman Maas had the support of a distinguished group of Marine Corps Reserve field grade officers. There were two colonels, Mark Sullivan and William G. Fay. Among the nine lieutenant colonels were Anthony J. D. Biddle, Clark W. Thompson and James Roosevelt—as well as Maas himself.

Congressman Maas often credited the Marine Corps Reserve Officers Association with furnishing the "driving force and spirit" behind his legislative efforts on behalf of the Marine Corps Reserve. It was typical of Mel Maas to speak with warm gratitude of the encouragement he had received, but there were reciprocal remarks from the gallant colleagues whose Marine Corps banner he had borne so faithfully in the halls of Congress. One of them, Richard

C. Mangrum, was on the roster of Marine Corps aviators who were classified as Marine "Regulars" until late 1924. Then, in 1929, First Lieutenant Maas was listed right next to Second Lieutenant Mangrum on the roster of Marine Corps Reserve aviators.

A tall, impressive officer, later to become Assistant Commandant of the Marine Corps, Lieut. Gen. Mangrum spoke with fervor of the legislative role that Congressman Maas performed so well, for the benefit of the country and the Corps. "We were fortunate to have so great a champion, right there in Congress," General Mangrum declared. "He almost singlehandedly kept the legislation moving. There was always that dynamic combination of dedication and terrific persistence!"

During several summers in the late 1930's, Lieut. Col. Maas was on active duty, teaching Marines to fly, at the Marine Air Base at Fort Ripley. The historic fort, located in central Minnesota, dates back to the "Indian pacification" days of 1849. One mile square at that time, it became a huge state-owned military reservation where Midwest troops assemble for field training every summer.

While Mel Maas was stationed at Ripley, Mrs. Maas and the girls had a cottage at Gull Lake, near Brainerd. "Pop"—as the girls loved to call him—did not join the family very often, but he had a devastating way of "keeping in touch." Whenever a plane flew low enough to "shiver the timbers" of the cottage, they knew "Pop" was up there thinking fondly of them. The girls still duck their heads involuntarily as they relive the "earthquake tremors" that rattled the roof and windows.

Sometimes "Pop" would land an amphibian near the dock at Gull Lake, but usually just to call out greetings and then zoom away again. His imagination was equal to every emergency. Once he dropped a note saying that he couldn't remember where he had put a check for five hundred dollars. If they found it in the cottage, they were supposed to signal him by spreading towels on the deck of the boat. The next time he flew over, he saw the towels and knew that he could stop worrying.

This man was not a dull parent. Obviously, he enjoyed life, and he wanted to share his thrills—all the lusty fruits of his imagination. He chose to live each day with a jaunty flair, a trait that is sometimes described as "Irish." Mel Maas had a proud, cocky way of looking at people and things—a "Sinn Feiner" personality like his grandfather's, perhaps. He did not deny his strain of healthy German blood, when it was called to his attention. But there was a wee bit of English ancestry in the family too. When it was mentioned, he said, "We don't talk about that." But, with all the contrary generosity of a typical Irishman, he did often mention that an Englishman named Sir Winston Churchill was probably "the great man of our age."

By 1939, all those weekly drills and periods of active duty on various flying fields had carried Mel Maas to the upper echelons of his branch of the service. On April 28, he became the youngest colonel in the Marine Corps. At that time he was assigned to the Fleet Marine Corps Reserve, and he was also in charge of Marine Corps Reserve Scouting Squadron Six at Wold-Chamberlain Field.

When President Roosevelt declared a state of national emergency in 1939, the Naval Reserve Act of 1938 overwhelmingly justified its existence. Without it, Colonel Wert notes, ". . . there would have been no Marine or Naval Reserves of any significant strength available for call-up." Due to Congressman Maas' indefatigable efforts, the Act provided the legislative framework for the vast expansion of the Marine Corps and Naval Reserve that later proved desperately necessary.

During every period of military strife, there have been hawks, doves, and moderates — with a wide range of conflicting and overlapping opinions. A strong faction of "America Firsters" believed that the United States should not concern itself with the Nazi or Fascist tyrannies that were threatening all the nations of Europe and northern Africa. Some Americans hoped that Hitler's ambitions would be satisfied if he were handed the small, proud democracy of Czechoslovakia on a silver platter. Others believed that the United States could continue to do business with Hitler, despite rumors of mass persecution of German Jews.

Aggressive tyranny seems to be a form of lust; success sharpens its appetite. Hitler and Mussolini were asking themselves, "Why should we stop when we are ahead? It is our destiny to conquer." Their war machines kept rolling with ominous precision.

In the oceans far out beyond the west coast of the United States, the Japanese were playing the same deadly military game, but it seemed farther away and of less consequence to Americans and Europeans.

Congressman Maas was not deeply concerned about ideologies or the eternal bickerings of arrogant old nations. He was worried about the ability of the United States to defend itself and its interests in a world bristling with modern warships, artillery, and bomber planes that could demolish the heart of a great city.

In the Nation's Capitol, debates on armaments seethed and simmered and sometimes erupted in hot exchanges of passion. There is a contemporary ring to some of the statements. In a discussion about Army and Navy appropriations on January 12, 1940, one member of the House of Representatives maintained: "We are a long way from a real emergency. Who are we afraid of? Russia? The Allies seem to be taking pretty good care of Germany, and they are a long way off."

Later in January, Congressman Maas took a somber view of sentiments of that type during a nationwide radio address on Town Meeting of the Air. Excerpts from that speech, which was published in the Congressional Record at the request of Congressman Carl Vinson, reveal Maas' coolheaded appraisal of the international situation:

". . . Both our foreign policy and the size of our Army and Navy are dependent upon constantly changing world conditions . . . The fundamental factor determining the size and character of our military establishment in the United States is the defense of the United States . . .

"What constitutes an adequate defense depends upon the forces with which it must cope. Therefore, our army and navy requirements change as the armies and navies of other nations change. If we are unprepared to resist any possible, or at least probable, aggressor, then we do not have adequate defenses . . ."

He pointed out that Japan had far exceeded the navy formula agreed upon after the Great War. "There is no need to fear that we are building any huge navy to implement some new overseas foreign policy . . . We are expanding only because the other navies of the world are expanding. To do otherwise is criminal folly." And even the present modest plans, he noted, would equip the nation to fight only a one-ocean war if attacked.

His final statement on adequate defense was a classic: "Let me close by reminding you that it is far better to have it and not need it than to need it and not have it."

Chapter Six

The Coral Reefs of Guam

The name of Congressman Maas is often associated with an historical debate concerning a small Pacific island in the Marianas. Situated about 1500 miles east of Manila, Guam is roughly thirty-two miles long, with a width that varies from four to ten miles. It was discovered by Ferdinand Magellan and claimed for Spain in 1521. In 1898, it was ceded to the United States at the conclusion of the Spanish-American War.

It is not known exactly when Melvin Maas "discovered" Guam, but he started giving it his assiduous attention in Congress as far back as 1930. As indicated by several discussions on the floor of the House in 1940, he was increasingly convinced that Guam was vital to future American influence in the Pacific.

On February 13, 1940, a Naval Appropriations Bill to finance the purchase and improvement of Hunters Point dry docks in San Francisco Bay—to provide a "major continental fleet base"—was being debated. At that time, the only dry docks on the Pacific coast large enough to accommodate major naval vessels with adequate repair facilities were located at Bremerton, Washington, more than eight hundred miles to the north.

After a thorough description of the situation, Congressman Ditter yielded twenty minutes to the gentleman from Minnesota. Mr. Maas spoke approvingly of the pending appropriations bill, but it was obvious that his attention was riveted on the coral-reefed island of Guam rather than San Francisco Bay. His great concern was a proposal "to remove the coral heads and make it possible to have proper sea runways for the planes which are using Guam."

That he had explored the historical, commercial and international political aspects of the situation was clearly evident: ". . . Guam has been in the possession of the United States for some forty years . . . We have maintained a naval base there during practically all that entire period . . . There was never any protest by Japan or anybody else. I cannot see what difference it would make whether Japan protests or not . . . Nobody has questioned our right to Guam or our occupancy of Guam. On the other hand, Japan occupies a great many surrounding islands to which there is a great question as to the right of Japan to be there at all. They are mandated islands, and under the mandate, and by treaty, Japan agreed not to fortify those islands, and we are certain, as a matter of fact, that they are fortified.

"I do not think Japan is going to get very mad at us and go to war because we take out some coral heads in the island of Guam. What we are asking to do is not making the slightest change in our policy over what we have been doing for forty years, which is to use the island of Guam both for the Navy and commercially. The Pan American Airways, which is an important commercial link with the Orient, uses Guam . . . That company has built an overnight hotel there. The increased size of the planes has made it dangerous to operate in Guam because of these coral heads . . ."

The subject of a United States withdrawal from the Philippines, when those islands were to be granted independence in 1946, was considered "inconsistent" with Congressman Maas' proposal for naval improvements on Guam. Should we not concentrate our national defense activities here in our own country and our nearby possessions, rather than "going way out into the Pacific?" On the contrary, Mr. Maas said, the very fact that we were getting out of the Philippines made it necessary to have other commercial and military "life lines" in that area. "The United States has to go to the Far East to get certain essential strategic raw materials, such as tin, rubber, tungsten and chromium. Without those essential raw materials, peacetime industry in this country would collapse."

The Congressman from Minnesota was emphatic about wanting to protect our economic interests in the Orient at that time, and as a progressive aviation man, he stressed that angle of it. "From the standpoint of the Pan American Airways operations, they are making a very valuable contribution to our commercial life. They would have to suspend operations if there were not some place in the approximate location of Guam where they could make a stop, for in their present state of development our planes today have not sufficient range to make the jump from Hawaii to the Philippines."

As for the squadron of American planes to be based in the Philippines until at least 1946, he noted that they had to be flown back to Hawaii for overhaul and needed to make a stop approximately where Guam is.

Inquiries revealed that the United States fleet was based at Pearl Harbor at that time. In his testimony, Congressman Maas pointed out that it would require weeks to get it into the Atlantic, either through the Panama Canal or around the Cape of Good Hope.

On that February day in 1940, he again affirmed his commitment to the idea of a two-ocean navy: "If ever we are threatened, it is going to be in both oceans at the same time. No single nation is going to be foolhardy enough to attack the United States or its essential interests alone, but a possible coalition of European and Oriental powers would be a very serious threat to us because we have only one fleet." Since it appeared that the United States could not afford a two-ocean navy, he believed the fortifying of Guam would be the best alternative.

Maas thought of Guam as a type of "early warning" station. "Guam is close enough to Japan so that planes based there can immediately observe the movement of the Japanese fleet." Aside from all that, "If we do not do what is provided in this bill, we will have to spend more money than the cost of this dredging in replacing planes that will get cracked up over there in Guam."

At times Mr. Maas was the object of sharp, probing questions. Mr. William Sutphin of New Jersey wanted to know if there were flying activities at Guam every day, a situation which might make the dredging of the harbor and eventual fortifications necessary.

Mr. Maas: "Not in the strict sense every day. I meant it is in use and available every day."

Mr. Sutphin: "Who is using it?"

Mr. Maas: "Pan American and our own navy."

Mr. Sutphin: "Our own navy? To what extent?"

Mr. Maas: "Whenever it is necessary to fly back and forth from the Philippines."

Mr. Sutphin: "The gentleman knows that when the P-13 squadron went out there the fleet was on the West Coast. That was last September, and that was their last activity out of Guam. This is February."

Mr. Maas: "But they have to come back for overhaul from time to time, and for training."

Mr. Sutphin: "Those twelve planes were through there in September."

Mr. Maas: "Yes. Pan American is using it constantly. The gentleman knows it."

Mr. Sutphin: "Yes, every day."

Mr. Maas: "The gentleman also knows that we maintained an active squadron of the Marine Corps there for many years without any protest from Japan."

Mr. Sutphin: "We do not maintain it there at the present time."

Mr. Maas: "No, it does not happen to be there at the present time, partly because of the difficulty of operating out of there with those coral reefs . . ."

The issue of strengthening Guam may have seemed of little consequence to most Congressmen, but the uneasiness of Mr. Maas was reflected in statements of this type on the floor of the House: ". . . Japan does not declare a war, and we want to know as far in advance as possible of any threatened danger." In answer to this query, "Do I correctly understand the gentleman to mean that if the Japanese fleet were to move in the direction of Guam on a practice cruise we would want to be notified of it?" Mr. Maas answered, "If a critical situation existed, as it may be getting to be now, you bet your life we would want to know it. We do not want the first knowledge of it to be some shells falling on Los Angeles, for instance, or the destruction of the Panama Canal."

With the luck of the Irish, and the cooperation of Mrs. Maas, Mel became the father of a leap-year baby that month. The proud Congressman was pictured in the newspapers with the lustily shrieking infant in his arms and his pockets crammed with cigars. One caption read, "Looks just like his father."

The House of Representatives celebrated the event, sandwiching it between a debate on Water Pollution Control in the United States Public Health Service and a request to extend some remarks on bituminous coal. Congressman Ludlow of Indiana did the honors, on February 29, 1940, with two and a half minutes of lofty rhetoric:

"Mr. Speaker, I do not think the House should adjourn today without appropriate recognition of a joyous event which occurred at 4:50 this morning at Providence Hospital when Melvin Joseph Maas Jr., or plain Joseph Maas, as the name will finally be determined, began his mundane career under favorable auspices, weight seven and one half pounds, muscles and vocal organs in fine trim, the first leap-year baby of the crop of 1940 to be born in the capital city of our nation.

"At last accounts the baby's father, our beloved colleague, the gentleman from Minnesota, Representative Melvin J. Maas, was doing well, in possession of all his faculties, proudly conscious of the honor that goes with the parenthood of an only son. When he came down from the stratosphere long enough to be interviewed he said he was uncertain whether he would bring up his boy to be a general in the Marine Corps or an admiral in the Navy.

"Though young in age and experience, Melvin Joseph, or Joseph, as the case may be, gave lusty evidence of his faith in the principles of the political party to which he belongs, which led his attendants rather to believe that he will be neither a general nor an admiral when he grows up, but a worthy member of this great legislative body in which his father has served so long and with such outstanding distinction.

"I hold in my hand a picture taken today of the gentleman from Minnesota, Representative Maas, with his offspring in his arms, and I defy anyone who looks at that picture to say that our colleague is not satisfied. Let us show our affectionate regard for the father and salute the son by giving both a rousing hand."

Mel and Katherine Maas were not the only members of the family who were delighted with the new addition. The three little girls were rapturous about having a baby brother. In the years ahead, little "Joe" would receive an abundance of tender, loving care.

The subject of national defense continued to be hotly debated throughout the year of 1940. On May 28, Mr. Vinson of Georgia introduced a bill for the "Construction of Naval Aircraft and Certain Public Works." The following is an illustration of the Vinson-Maas "legislative partnership" to which Charlie Jordan referred.

"Mr. Speaker," the gentleman from Georgia said, "I move that the House resolve itself into the Committee of the whole House to authorize the construction or acquisition of naval aircraft, the construction of certain public works, and for other purposes; and pending that motion I ask unanimous consent that general debate may be limited to two hours, to be equally divided and controlled by the gentleman from Minnesota (Mr. Maas) and myself."

Mr. Vinson spoke eloquently and with a spirit of urgency. "Now . . . one of the main purposes is to provide in the very shortest time possible 16,000 aviators for the Navy." He recalled that, in 1935, Congress enacted what is known as the aviation cadet bill, providing for flight training of Naval and Marine Corps reserves at Pensacola, Florida. To expedite the training program, expanded facilities were necessary. "Just as soon as this bill becomes a law, a deficiency appropriation to provide the money will be asked for. When this program has been completed and the 10,000 planes have been purchased and the 16,000 aviators obtained, it will entail an expenditure of approximately $1,150,000,000. If Congress and the American people but adhere to the advice of the Father of Our Country—no entangling alliances, and in peacetime prepare for war—this Republic will never perish from the face of the earth." As he finished on that high note, Mr. Vinson received a spontaneous ovation from his colleagues.

Many opinions were heard in the House that day, and some of them sound almost bizarre when viewed from the latter half of the Twentieth Century—and with the benefit of hindsight.

Congressman Fish of New York went on record with this isolationist appeal: ". . . We are in the midst of war hysteria, of fear, and a dread of war. Many columnists in the East, internationalists and interventionists, like Kaltenborn, Lippmann, Dorothy Thompson and Frederick Wile, are every day deluging the American people with war propaganda, war hysteria . . . Many good Americans believe today that the Congress has failed in its duty to provide an adequate navy, that we are as defenseless and as helpless as Abyssinia, Poland, China, Holland, or Belgium, and that we are about to be attacked . . ."

The British had a "close call" on that May day in 1940. Congressman Fish favored asking England to liquidate a part of its war debt by turning over to us "those islands off our shores that rightly belong to us — Bermuda, Nassau, Jamaica, and the West Indies, so that we could use those islands as air bases and submarine bases for the protection of our own country."

Some of the Congressmen argued that the 1940 theater of war had shifted from the earth to the sky —that air strength would be our best safeguard. Others applied the Monroe Doctrine to all coast lines of the North and South American continents. There were pleas for more planes and airfields in the United States, with Congressman Johnson of Oklahoma calling attention to ". . . disclosures of 'fifth column' activities, spies, saboteurs, and other subversive activities along the Mexican border . . . With our vast resources in the Southwest, and particularly considering our great oil fields, coal fields, lead and zinc mines, we cannot afford to permit them to go unprotected from any potential enemy, whether they be Communists, Fascists, Nazis, or 'fifth column' spies, who might come over the Mexican border riding their Trojan horses."

Although Mr. Maas acknowledged that the defense bill in that session of Congress did not include provisions for facilities outside the continental United States, both he and Mr. Vinson made it clear that the subject of fortifying Guam might be brought up in the next session. Said the Congressman from Minnesota, ". . . I think history will demonstrate that one of the worst votes ever cast in this House was the vote against fortifying Guam. When this nation says to the world that we are not going to defend any part of our territory, it is a sad state of affairs."

Mr. Maas predicted, optimistically, that the rejected bill to fortify Guam would pass overwhelmingly when it was presented again for further consideration.

Mr. Ralph Church of Illinois asked him, "How long would it take to fortify Guam?"

Mr. Maas said, "You could make a Gibraltar out of Guam in less than five years. But . . . if you would dredge the coral heads out of the harbors so seaplanes could land and take off and put enough Marines over there with proper equipment, they would hold that island against Japan or anyone else for a long time. . . . You could prepare Guam to withhold a considerable siege in a matter of six months or a year."

The subject of aviation training for 16,000 men was explored. Mr. Vorys of Ohio asked if the Navy "proposed to give an all-around training to all pilots." He wondered "if it would not be better to train these men to be specialists in flying a particular type of ship, if by so doing we would not train them more rapidly and keep them in condition more economically."

Mr. Maas answered, "I may say to the gentleman from Ohio that that is exactly what the Navy is now doing . . . The primary training is the same, that is fundamental. Then they are divided up for tactical training when some learn to fly the big boats, some the pontoon planes for duty on battleships and cruisers, and others go to land-planes, which is the type of plane used on the carriers . . ."

The gentleman from Ohio responded, "I am delighted to know that."

Miss Sumner of Illinois asked an almost clairvoyant question. "Does the gentleman know of any potential enemy except Japan that might be preparing to fight the United States within the next year and a half?"

"I do not know," Mr. Maas replied. "I am no seer. All I know is that America is the garden spot of the world, and it is hardly feasible to believe that the hungry wolves of the rest of the world will stay out of our garden unless we build a doggone good high picket fence; and that is what I want to see done now by passing this bill."

Mr. James Van Zandt of Pennsylvania introduced a new angle by stating that, "We are now very active in building up our national defenses, and are spending a tremendous amount of money on them. I wonder if the gentleman can give us any assurance that after this war is over, probably in the next few weeks we may find ourselves playing our part in an armament-reduction program?"

The Congressman from Minnesota drew a burst of applause when he answered, "I feel that I can say positively that not within the memory of any of the members of this House shall we ever again see any of our American ships sunk by a treaty. From now on we will build such a navy as we need for our protection, independent of what anybody else does, and then we will maintain it forevermore."

Some of the arguments and sentiments sound ambiguous in a later era, but it can be assumed that "doves" and "hawks" are not a brand-new phenomenon in the United States.

The $1,150,000,000 Naval Appropriations Bill (House Resolution 9848) was passed on that day in May 1940, with no provisions for improving the harbor at Guam. The final tally was 402 yeas, and one nay.

That was the month of the gallant but ill-fated Dunkirk expedition by the British. By the end of the month, the Nazi conquest of Europe was reaching alarming proportions. After swallowing Czechoslovakia in one quick gulp, Hitler's hordes had been sweeping into Poland, Norway, Denmark, the Netherlands, Belgium and Luxemburg. Late in June 1940, German tanks pounded relentlessly around the French underground fortress called the Maginot Line, and the Vichy government signed an armistice of surrender with the Nazis.

Mel Maas was appalled about the European situation, but he suffered his worst "porcupine prickles" of apprehension when he studied the area dominated by the inscrutable Japanese.

Would Japan prove a threat to the United States? The Minnesota Congressman did not know the answer, and the Japanese surely were not taking him into their confidence. Obviously his uneasiness about Japanese imperialistic ambitions was based as much on intuition as on hard facts. He was trying to warn the country of a very possible danger, without evidence straight from Tokyo—and sometimes it was so frustrating that he erupted in uncharacteristically harsh language.

As a member of the House Naval Affairs Committee, Mr. Maas always had some classified facts in his mind. This, Colonel William McCahill has pointed out, can be a slight disadvantage to a Congressman who is "speaking off the cuff." If he gets in the middle of a hot debate and then starts wondering if he is accidentally citing classified material, he may suddenly swerve in another direction and end up sounding as though he is contradicting himself. Considering the belligerent temper of the world at that time, the United States was in no mood to tell potential enemies its secrets either.

During that summer Congressman Maas made a proposal that will appeal to Americans who are concerned about unpaid war debts. On July 27, 1940, he suggested that the United States send a naval force to Martinique to escort the French aircraft carrier

Bearn, with one hundred airplanes aboard, to a safe United States port. He was of the opinion that the United States would have legal grounds for such action because the situation at Martinique, where British warcraft were watching to prevent the Bearn from falling into German hands, might result in hostilities within the American hemisphere safety zone.

"If we don't get the planes, Hitler or the British will," Congressman Maas said. "We ought to bring them and the carrier to the United States and deduct the value from France's debt to the United States."

Always an "insurgent" who cared more about the issue than the party label, Congressman Maas was the only Western Republican who voted for the conscription law that year.

Grace Tully, President Roosevelt's secretary, still remembers that period in history. The President, who enjoyed teasing her, said she'd better get ready —they might be drafting women too.

"They won't need to draft me," Grace told him. "I'll enlist in the Marines!"

Chapter Seven

A Greater World War

The war shadows over America had been darkening, month after month, while isolationists kept trying to talk the tempest away, but Congressman Maas kept helping to prepare the country for the struggle ahead. Keeping in close contact with America's European allies was an important part of the preparedness picture.

During that period of tension, it was determined that a party of Congressmen should confer with Prime Minister Winston Churchill — and perhaps even with the King of England—and other heads of state.

At the same time, a young Marine officer named Wallace M. Greene Jr., who would later become Commandant of the Marine Corps, was ordered to proceed to Africa with another Marine officer. They and the Congressional party—which included Representative Maas—were all on the same aircraft, an old Pan American seaplane. Miserable flying weather, all the way, buffeted the plane so badly that it was necessary at one point to make a forced landing in the Azores.

The Congressional group had been assigned to a separate section of the plane; and during the last night, carbon monoxide fumes leaked into their compartment. There was moaning and groaning and perhaps even some gnashing of teeth. General Maas was sick too, but Major Greene observed with interest that he helped his colleagues to pull themselves together and got them organized to debark from the plane with a commendable amount of Congressional dignity when it landed.

All those who believed that war was inevitable were "shaping up" for the storm ahead, but it looked as though Mel Maas had already had his Great War. In November 1940, the Colonel received notification that "Marine Reserve Scouting Squadron Six, of which you are the commanding officer, will be mobilized and ordered to active duty at the Naval Air Station, San Diego, California, on or about December 16, 1940. The Major General is of the opinion that your continuance in the important position you now hold in the Congress of the United States will be of greater value to the national defense than active duty in the Marine Corps. In view of the above, orders will be issued affecting your transfer to the Volunteer Marine Corps Reserve upon the mobilization of Marine Reserve Scouting Squadron Six."

That was an order to make Congressman-Colonel Maas pace the floor of his lovely home on Dale Drive in a fit of frustration! No healthy Marine officer would want his men to go on without him—leaving him in drydock. He was only forty-two years old and in the prime of his life—and fit to be tied!

Mel Maas' children laugh as they recall the zeal with which "Pop" refused to let any fireside barnacles grow on him. About the middle of July 1941, he turned up for aviation duty aboard the USS Enterprise as an "observer" on the staff of the Commander of the Air Battle Force. This neat trick was somehow accomplished through the courtesy of Admiral William F. Halsey who had assigned the Marine Colonel from Minnesota to a tour of temporary duty "in connection with the flight of patrol planes to Midway, Johnston, Palmyra, and Wake islands." In August, the effervescent Colonel Maas was assigned to the Aviation Unit, Ninth Reserve District.

In spite of some military "commuting," Mel Maas did attach great importance to his responsibilities as a Congressman. The record reveals that he was often on "active duty" on the floor of the House where he introduced a number of resolutions—some of which would greatly benefit the welfare of the armed forces.

On December 8, 1941, historic House Joint Resolution 254 was read by the Speaker of the House, Sam Rayburn. Solemnly intoning the words that spelled death to peace for the United States, Mr. Rayburn declared that "a state of war exists between Japan and the United States," and authorized the President to employ the entire naval and military forces of the Government to carry on the war. Japan had invaded Indo-China in September. On December

7, 1941, the Japanese unleashed a vicious aerial bombardment on the U. S. Pacific fleet in Pearl Harbor, and simultaneously launched air and land attacks against the Philippines, Guam, Midway, Hong Kong, Thailand and several other areas from which they wanted Western influence expelled.

Declarations of war against Japan's allies, Germany and Italy, followed on December 11, 1941. No longer would civilization refer to the cataclysm of 1914-1918 as "The Great War." Until the bombing in the Pacific in 1941, the world had never been clasped by so fiery a girdle of warfare.

On May 28, 1940, Congressman Maas had stated in the House, "You could prepare Guam to withhold a considerable siege in a matter of six months or a year." Guam was one of the first strategic islands attacked by the Japanese, and it fell in less than two weeks. Only on Corregidor and Bataan, where Philippine and American defenses had been strengthened by a military and social partnership, would the enemy's victorious progress be retarded for more than four remarkable months.

Every time he thought of Guam, Mel Maas felt his Irish blood boiling up. He knew the Japanese would waste no time "digging in" and fortifying all those islands in the Southeast Pacific—and that it could take countless months of relentless warfare and thousands of young American lives to break the Nipponese grip on each island that had been confiscated almost overnight. Both Nazi Germany and Japan had proved that aggression is easy—if there is nothing in the way.

The Marine Reserves were sometimes called "weekend warriors," but they had been ruggedly trained in the Corps tradition and were ready for action. The peacetime Marine Reserve suddenly evaporated, merging itself with the Regular forces on the farflung battlefields of the world. They were all Marines together.

The Army, Navy and Air Force performed with commendable distinction, but any history of the Pacific theater is top-heavy with references to the Marine valor—with its traditional blend of dedicated doggedness and cussedness—on bloody beachheads and in bleak island strongholds all along the line from Guadalcanal and Okinawa to the Philippines.

Commandant Wallace Greene has noted that the jungle warfare techniques learned in the Philippines and Latin American "banana wars" have continued to be a part of Marine Corps training and that they proved invaluable during World War II and in later guerrilla warfare operations.

As a Marine, Colonel Melvin Maas performed during World War II with disciplined obstinacy. If there were a war going on, he wanted to be in the thick of it—where the aircraft zoomed, and ground forces hurtled forward, and the fleet rode high on the bounding main. The fleet? After Pearl Harbor, that was an extremely sore spot with Colonel Maas.

Mel Maas was active in as many places as possible during World War II. To achieve victory, that pathetic mass of sunken ships at Pearl Harbor would need to be replaced. Maas would never consider the possibility of defeat, no matter how formidable the handicaps. Even the word "retreat" is not recognized in the Marine training program.

Charlie Jordan remembers that "Congressman Maas and Congressman Vinson were often busy on Capitol Hill from early morning until late at night during World War II—they got more appropriations for aircraft carriers and naval equipment than ever before."

Maas was also active on the House Committee on Naval Affairs that was investigating the soundness of the National Defense Program. One hearing, held in late May 1942, dealt with alleged "irregularities" in a private company that appeared to have cut some ethical corners, perhaps in an effort to speed up its World War II production lines. Among the witnesses for the company was a former officer receiving retirement pay from the U. S. Government while serving as president of the private concern—which had contracts with the Government.

In the course of the investigation, the company's financial dealings were subjected to relentless scrutiny, and Mr. Maas often revealed by his questions that he knew his way around in the world of stocks, bonds, and tax liens.

Hour after hour, the counsel for the Government played a major offensive role, delivering rapierlike thrusts and receiving cooly defensive answers from those who were being investigated.

Whenever he spoke, Mr. Maas showed both fairness toward the witnesses and concern on behalf of the Government. At one point during a rambling cross-examination dealing with shipbuilding contracts, possible price fixing, and questionable manipulation of subcontracts and purchases of materials, he told a witness, ". . . I suggest that you answer the questions so as not to leave inferences. There have been altogether too many inferences in this hearing already."

Maas sounded more like a mediator than a relentless inquisitor, but he probed deeply. During one exchange, when he began to sound extremely persistent about the value of a stock issue, he paused to say, "I am just seeking information. I am not trying to argue with the witness." Then he went right back to the same subject until he had a satisfactory answer. Sifting through the pages of questions, it is apparent that Mr. Maas believed in the freedom of free enterprise, but he also believed that all citizens had a "moral obligation" to conduct their national defense activities with both speed and patriotic integrity.

The final verdict in that case was not as dramatic as all the verbal fire and brimstone that preceded it. The company was declared innocent of sinister motives toward the Government.

In addition to the fact that President Roosevelt was a Democrat and Congressman Maas was a Republican, they had several other areas of disagreement. The President believed that Congressmen should remain constantly in Washington during the wartime emergency. However, Mel Maas was a man with at least two hats, and he had an exasperating habit of putting his Marine Corps "cover" on his head and dashing off to war.

In the summer of 1942, Colonel Maas somehow managed to stay a running jump ahead of the President's "come home" order. During two periods in July and August, he was on temporary duty with a Marine Detachment aboard the USS Saratoga far out in the Pacific—so somebody knew where he was. Since he served as an intelligence officer part of that time, he might have developed some "invisible man" tactics.

Colonel Maas was where he wanted most to be that August, on the staff of Admiral Frank J. Fletcher in the Solomon Islands during the first "island-hopping" engagements of the Pacific War. History has recorded the fierce assaults by the 1st Division of the Marine Corps on the beachheads of Guadalcanal, Tulagi, and several smaller islands. The Japanese launched fierce counteroffensives against all the Allied forces, pouring reinforcements into Guadalcanal, bombing and strafing from the air, and sinking four Allied cruisers in a "sneak attack." It was a bloody, costly operation for both sides. The Japanese were defeated in a two-day naval battle in November, but "mopping-up" operations continued into February of the next year.

Although Congressmen were supposed to stay out of danger zones, it was not enough for Mel Maas to be a protected observer behind the lines. He wanted to strike some personal blows for victory, even if he had to use unorthodox methods. It was a cinch he wouldn't come home "empty-handed" if he could help it.

In the early fall of 1942, New Guinea was the battleground, and Colonel Melvin J. Maas was very much there — still dodging those orders to come home. The truant Congressman would finally return to Washington—but he would take with him, by command of General Douglas MacArthur, the Army Silver Star and the following citation:

"For gallantry in action over New Guinea on September 3, 1942: When word was received at Port Moresby, New Guinea, that the enemy warcraft had put into Milne Bay and that heavy ground fighting had broken out during the night of September 2-3, Colonel Maas volunteered to accompany a crew of one of several planes on a reconnaissance of the area, acting as observer and manning the port gun as auxiliary gunner. On finding that the enemy had left Milne Bay and that the ground fighting had become desultory, the plane immediately left in search for the enemy warcraft. It located and dropped food and supplies to an isolated outpost on the northern coast of New Guinea, searched out enemy airdromes, machine-gunning one, and continued a determined and difficult search for the ships, flying over eight hours under extremely unfavorable weather conditions. This voluntary and aggressive effort on the part of Colonel Maas to assist in any capacity in the combat reconnaissance of an important area occupied by the enemy is worthy of the finest tradition of our fighting forces."

"This voluntary and aggressive effort . . ." Those words were typical of Melvin Maas, the man who always wanted to be on active duty. And it was typical of General Douglas MacArthur, with his appreciation of dramatic exploits, to salute the Marine officer with an Army Silver Star.

Maas always recalled, with a twinkle in his eye, that there was a verbal rebuke attached to that award.. MacArthur reprimanded him for engaging in aerial combat when he was merely supposed to be acting as an "observer" and for risking government property by using a medium bomber as a dive bomber to strafe that enemy airfield. But Mel knew that he had to be resourceful, and he didn't have a dive bomber handy.

The Army Silver Star was added to the personal collection of awards and decorations that the dauntless Marine Colonel had already received. His cherished Victory Medal with Aviation clasp signified that he had been a daring young man in a flying machine during World War I. In 1934, he received the Organized Marine Corps Medal. When it was politely suggested, in 1940, that being a Congressman was more important than continuing as Commander of Marine Reserve Scouting Squadron 6, the Secretary of the Navy magnanimously saluted the Marine pilot with a Letter of Commendation and the Reserve Special Commendation Ribbon. In 1941, Maas was presented with the Marine Corps Reserve Ribbon for his ten years of service in the Marine Corps Reserve, and the American Defense Service Medal with

Fleet Clasp for his service aboard the USS Enterprise.

By the end of September, Colonel Maas had again made connections with his family and his seat in Congress.

Chapter Eight

A Lovely Home on Dale Drive

Although his colorful public life receives more attention, Mel Maas had a fascinating family life too—especially in the home on Dale Drive in Silver Spring, Maryland, a northern suburb of the Capitol City. The Maas family had lived in two other houses in the area, but had not managed to feel permanently attached to them. There were occasional discussions about the sort of home they would like to find some day.

Little Patricia took those conversations very seriously. She developed a mania for going through "open houses" wherever she found them, but she was not easy to please. There was one place on Dale Drive that gladdened her heart whenever she saw it. She would slow down and give it a wistful look. "I had my eyes on the house for quite awhile," she recalls.

It was a tall house, with a handsome porch on which stately columns ascended almost to the roof. Crowning the dignified doorway was a fan-shaped window set with intricate panes of glass, and a similar window decorated the base of the second story. The lawn sloped gracefully toward the street in front, and there was a heavily wooded area on one side. Pat would sigh and go on her way. She had very good taste in houses, but someone else was living there.

One day she slowed her bicycle and stopped with a little gasp of surprise. There was a "For Sale" sign on the lawn of her dream house! She remembers that she had been playing and probably had smudges on her face. Considering that she didn't look like a "paying customer" at her age, she appreciated the courtesy with which the owners conducted her through their lovely home. They undoubtedly basked in her enthusiasm, because she found the place as impressive on the inside as on the outside.

The little girl raced her bicycle home and wasted no time describing all the charms of the house on Dale Drive—the entrance hall with a staircase curving down one side, the spacious rooms, the huge upstairs and downstairs screened porches at the back, the fireplaces and lovely hardwood floors. She was so persuasive that her parents decided to look at that fabulous place.

Pat could tell that her mother was "sold" almost immediately. Congressman Maas scrutinized the house and grounds carefully. He seemed favorably impressed at the time, but he didn't say much. Pat held her breath. The next day her father came home and announced that he had bought the house on Dale

Drive. "That's the way he did things," Pat said. It was the dramatic way.

This was the home in which young Joe would grow from babyhood almost to young manhood. Pat remembers sharing her room first with her older sister and then with the younger one—depending on which one was left at home.

The new house brought Congressman Maas very close to his family. In fact, he could scarcely tear himself away. He had an almost fantastic number of projects going, during those years. The adjoining wooded area, he decided, should be cleared and landscaped. This, as a matter of course, would provide a huge stack of wood for the fireplaces in the living room and basement. The enormous woodpile became a landmark in the back yard. There was a pint-sized ravine after many of the huge trees were removed, and thirty loads of "fill" were ordered. Mel Maas wheelbarrowed all that dirt to the places where it was needed. While he was trying to get the lawn in shape, he took time to build a playhouse for little Joe in the newly cleared area.

When he was busy with chores of this type, the Congressman often indulged in outlandish haberdashery. There was one outfit that the young people of the Maas family remember with affectionate horror. Because he hated to throw "good" things away, "Pop" insisted on having his regulation trousers cut off and hemmed, when they were worn out at the knees. With the abbreviated pants he wore a faded olive T-shirt. On his feet were sturdy Marine boots, and he topped the whacky ensemble off with a tropical cork helmet. Since he couldn't be without them, there were cigars bulging out of every pocket. About that time, he was being described as "stout and stocky" in his military record.

There is no doubt that Congressman Maas looked every inch a hard worker. One day, when he was mowing the lawn, a shiny car slowed down and stopped. A sympathetic dowager leaned out and beckoned to him. "My good man, are they treating you all right here?" she asked.

"Sometimes it gets pretty bad," he admitted, removing his cork helmet and mopping his brow.

"If you are interested in making a change, I would like very much to have you work for me," she told him.

After she had driven away, the Congressman strolled into the house and told his family about the unexpected offer. At the end of the narrative, he paused thoughtfully and said, "I think I'll take that job."

The house on Dale Drive inspired Mel Maas in the same way that a block of marble stimulated the imagination of Michelangelo. Over quite a period of years—when he wasn't continuously busy in Congress, or off to the war—he had a great batch of projects under development.

He set up a small office for himself in one room of the large basement, and he extended the basement out into the back yard in order to have both a workshop and a garage. He constructed shelves and racks all over the place, to hold his tools and other carpentering equipment. Part of the phenomenal collection of empty cigar boxes—which had multiplied through the years because he hated to throw "good" things away—were made into drawers for "filing" nuts, bolts and nails. The others were carefully taken apart and the pieces stacked up for future reference. At the rate he was smoking cigars, he might be able to build another house after awhile.

Presently the new workroom began to bulge with tools and equipment for projects that were being planned, and the residue overflowed into the adjacent garage. Mel Maas asked himself if garages were really necessary. He extended the driveway farther into the back yard, with space for two cars to be parked side by side. "After that," young Joe recalls, "the cars were always parked right there—not in the garage." During the cementing of the driveway, the Congressman added a crowning touch—a special little niche for the garbage pails, under a tumbling cascade of spiraea bushes.

The Maas family loved the lawn with its huge old trees. They added pink and white dogwood and saucy crimson azaleas. It was a pleasure on hot summer nights to look out on the lighted lawn from the screened porch upstairs. Trust the Congressman to cope with the "tropical heat and humidity!" He built a rack to hold a huge fan, so the upstairs porch was cool for living and sleeping all summer long.

Some of his experimental wiring indicates that Mel Maas was no expert, but he surely was electricity-conscious. He put a small, round pane of glass —not much larger than a silver dollar—in the door of the fruit cellar. There was no danger the light would be left burning for a couple of days, with that peephole to snitch on absentminded fruit-cellar visitors.

Young Joe Maas remembers when he used to ride "horseback" on the big green oil tank in the basement. Still in use in the laundry room are the large washer and dryer that "Pop" smuggled into the house to surprise Mrs. Maas one Christmas Eve.

Mel Maas had to keep coming and going, with his crowded schedule in Congress, his Marine Corps Reserve activities, and the dozens of organizations to which he belonged. But that house on Dale Drive was his refuge and his castle.

He was not a "lord and master" type of father. He encouraged the children to debate their own points of view with him. When his wife became perturbed about the lustiness of some of the discussions, Mel would say, "Oh, we're just clarifying an issue."

Little Joe—Melvin Jr—went through the normal mischievous stage. He still has fond memories of the time that he and one of his friends aimed two dozen eggs at the side of the house, trying to hit an upstairs bathroom window. They had already cleaned off the dribbling mess by the time Joe's father came home, and he thought it was funnier than Mrs. Maas had.

Mel often drank his coffee in the pleasant living room after dinner. He would settle down in one of his favorite chairs near the fireplace, like a country squire, and watch the news on TV.

Mrs. Maas absolutely would not allow any TV

wrestling bouts to be viewed in the living room, so the two men of the household would retire to Mel's office in the basement and watch the grunters and groaners on the other set. Even though he knew it wasn't "for real," Joe said his father would reach a feverish pitch of excitement during those wrestling bouts. "Pop" was stimulating company and a great pal to Joe during those growing-up years.

The Maas children have many fond recollections of their adolescent years, but Sandy, the youngest daughter, has one bitter-sweet memory of the time her father tried to teach her to drive. The engine died, and she froze stiff at the wheel in traffic. "Pop" tried coaxing, in reasonable tones. Then, with horns blaring around them, he began to sound like an embarrassed drill instructor—but Sandy couldn't budge a muscle. Finally her frantic father raced around the car, shoved his little daughter to the other side of the seat, and took control of the steering wheel himself.

Mel Maas tried never to use any profanity around ladies, although the urge must have been strong that day. Once, when he hit his finger with a hammer in the workshop and exploded with several strong words, he suddenly noticed that Sandy was there. As both a gentleman and a father, he apologized profusely.

All of the Maas family took a keen interest in the Congressman's activities on Capitol Hill. He kept a diary, day after day, for several decades. It was a handy reference source when there were discussions or arguments about the dates or particulars of certain pieces of legislation—which there were, in that lively household.

Being a farsighted legislator was important to Congressman Maas. Joe remembers the pride he took in the plaque that he had hanging in his office. It read: "Politicians think of the next election, but statesmen think of the next generation."

Congressman Maas was strongly opposed to nepotism. He paid Pat's salary when she worked in his office one summer. "And it wasn't much," she recalled with a grin.

The children grew up knowing that their father was a man of instant eloquence, but he put Sandy through some tense moments when he took her along to a Memorial Day ceremony at Arlington Cemetery one year. Sandy knew that her father was scheduled to deliver the main address at the majestic white Memorial Amphitheater, but she also knew that he didn't have any notes with him. He seemed blithely unconcerned about the program ahead, even though its success depended upon him.

Sandy had a bloodcurdling vision of her father—standing up there in front of all those important people—trying desperately to think of something to say. The calmer he seemed, the more frantic Sandy grew. She wasn't soothed by his final assurance, "I'll get some ideas when I see the audience."

When they arrived at the amphitheater, Mel Maas went around shaking hands and chatting casually, while his youngest daughter had the jitters.

Sandy said she needn't have worried. Her father

got up and gave a wonderful speech, full of patriotism, wit and human warmth. It was agreed, among those who heard him talk often, that Mel Maas could deliver an inspiring speech lasting anywhere from two minutes to two hours—extemporaneously.

The Congressman had an exhausting schedule, especially during the war years in Congress, and it seems as though he should have slept long and heavily at night. Instead, he suffered from insomnia. Often he would get up in the darkness and sit in thoughtful meditation in the living room. One night, when Sandy came home late from a date, she was worried that he had been waiting up for her. He cut short her rapid-fire excuses, not wanting her to feel that he didn't trust her. "I just got up because I couldn't sleep," he explained, as he urged her upstairs to bed and then returned to his solitary vigil. His was a restless mind, not easily given to tranquility by day or by night.

On another night, Congressman Maas was awake and pacing the floor—but not from insomnia. Most Washingtonians take their blizzards seriously, but Pat had decided that "a little snow couldn't keep a Minnesota girl from going to a dance!" The sparks were almost flying while she and her father "discussed" that subject at length, and finally he told her to use her own judgment.

Pat's date was driving, and he had to take everyone else home first—and those were the days of temperamental windshield wipers, when they had to keep cleaning the windshield off with salt. It really had been a nasty blizzard. Pat had plenty of excuses, but they availed her nothing. She was deprived of dating privileges for the next two weeks.

Chapter Nine

Home Front and Battle Front

One day in 1943, the news filtered over to Marine Headquarters that some scoundrel on Capitol Hill favored adding ladies' units to the famed "Leatherneck" branch of the service which had long been considered "For Men Only." When the news reached the startled ears of Commandant Thomas Holcomb, he grabbed the telephone and called a Congressman who ought to know the score.

"Do you know that we might have to take women into the Marine Corps?" he asked in alarm.

"Yes," Mel Maas admitted. "I introduced that legislation."

"The Marine Corps will be ruined!" his superior officer boomed. "Our friendship is over." He meant it at the time, but he later accepted the feminine infiltration with good grace and approval.

Short-term enlistments were actually what Colonel Maas had in mind—not lifetime careers—but he found that women are likely to make their own decisions on matters of that type. He knew several charming ladies, including his own daughter Patricia, who presently joined the Marines and stayed in.

Mel Maas' change of heart was most apparent almost ten years later when he wrote a letter recommending that "the regulations of the military departments be modified so that women members of the reserve will not be discharged from the reserve permanently by reason of having dependents." If the status of the dependents had changed or if arrangements for care of children had been made, many of these women would be "critically needed in case of mobilization." In addition to giving consideration to women in the Marine Corps, he sponsored legislation to give officer ratings to all nurses on active duty in the armed forces.

Approximately three hundred "Marinettes" served in the Marine Corps during World War I. With so coy a name, a phobia may have developed, because it was almost twenty-three years before anyone said much about women Marines again.

In 1948, the Women's Armed Integration Act gave women Marines regular status. Women Marine officers and enlisted personnel are now on active duty all over the world.

Pat Maas went first to Carleton College at Northfield, Minnesota. As a Marine officer candidate, she used to ask her bewildered father to let her out of the car a block from the barracks. She wanted no favors or wisecracks about her possible relationship to an upper echelon officer in the Marine Corps—but the question did keep popping up. At last there came a day when Mel Maas needed a car at Marine Headquarters to take him to an appointment, and the driver asked him, "Are you Captain Maas' father?" When he told the story at home, he sounded very proud that he could claim to be Captain Maas' father—and Patricia felt as though she had "finally arrived."

In his attitude about the war in the Pacific, Congressman Maas had come tearing back to Washington with blood in his eye and loaded for bear. In 1944 he campaigned on the side of the anti-Administration forces who blamed the disaster at Pearl Harbor on the party in power. There was evidence that militant Japan had included the Hawaiian Islands in its immediate Asian-conquest pattern and that proper precautions might have been taken in time. On the Administration side there was also evidence of shock that the Nipponese actually had dared to strike at American territorial islands that were closer to Los Angeles than to Tokyo. Almost forgotten now, it was a lesson of historical importance. The controversy raged for years, and sometimes in the heat of argument, people seemed to forget that it was the Japanese who had launched the "sneak attack."

Mel Maas, along with Carl Vinson, had fought so hard on the floor of Congress to build up a mighty U. S. Navy. In addition to all the human and property damage, eight American battleships and ten other vessels had become ravaged hulks in the waters of Pearl Harbor. It grieved Congressman Maas that his impassioned warnings about the destructive power of military planes had been taken so lightly. Furthermore, he believed that President Roosevelt was losing the war in the Pacific by concentrating the heaviest offensive in Europe and Africa first.

That was why, in 1944, the irrepressible Congressman went from platform to platform telling his constituents, "If you are going to vote for Roosevelt, don't vote for me!"

They didn't. He lost by a slim margin.

Perhaps it was just as well that Mel Maas could don his Marine Corps uniform again and feel free to concentrate on the war effort.

With characteristic aplomb, Colonel Maas sent this message to the Commandant of the Marine Corps on the morning of January 3, 1945: "It is requested that I be ordered to immediate active duty." The mail must have moved fast in those days. That same afternoon he was detailed to "duty involving flying with Aeronautic Organizations of the Marine Corps as a Naval Aviator and Pilot."

No matter where he happened to be, Mel Maas made a tremendous impact on people—even if they started out as strangers. Early in May 1945, a lady named Mrs. Lynch Steiner met the Colonel at the California home of her good friends, Betty and Roy Smith. Mrs. Steiner's husband, a Marine Corps pilot, was going through two weeks of training at Camp Pendleton prior to being sent overseas for his second tour of duty. Suzanne Steiner still remembers that "It was an evening I'm sure none of us will ever forget—four hours of being completely fascinated by a man whose name meant nothing to us prior to that night, but one we will remember as long as we live."

Mrs. Steiner noted that the evening got off to a rather slow start with the usual exchange of pleasantries, "... but after dinner Colonel Maas proceeded to discuss what he thought would happen after the war was over which, at that time, was closer than any of us dared hope." They were startled when he predicted that the United States would be confronted by an extremely hostile Communist Russia and that it might be wise to forestall aggressive Soviet ambitions before it was too late.

Mrs. Steiner said that these remarks about "our good friend Russia who was helping us win the war," were devastating enough—"but when he started to tell us that our most threatening enemy would be China, you can well imagine how disbelieving we were. He said China would definitely turn Communistic and might slowly but surely try to take over the Far East, and unless they were stopped at their first attempt, they would probably succeed.

"He went on to explain how rich the Far East was in almost untapped resources, how vital were the trade routes to the free world and how control of both would make China one of the most powerful countries in the world, while our dwindling resources would sap our strength to a dangerous degree." With the United States at war against two other enemies at that time, it sounded "farfetched" even to consider "the unlikely chances of a 'war-tired' Russia and a 'poverty-stricken' China contemplating the possibility of ruling the world.

"The strange part about the whole evening," Mrs. Steiner reported, "was that no one argued with him which is a good indication of what a dynamic and convincing person he was—and as history has unfolded, what a terribly wise person . . ."

Mel Maas was basically a happy man who shunned pessimism and often said that international disputes should be resolved at the treaty table and not on the battlefield. He wanted to have all the faith in the world in his fellow men. Even when it seemed inevitable that a Communist government would be established in China, he was heard to say that he hoped it would not happen. He was a man of many moods—all of them dramatic and discerning—but perhaps his predictions were most accurate when anxiety sharpened his vision.

Only a few days after that visit, the war in Europe ended with the surrender of Germany and the suicide of Adolph Hitler. It was not long before Russia swooped down on her neighbors and made Communist satellites of them, and Berlin became a divided city.

By the middle of May 1945, Mel Maas was outward bound for the Pacific again. A medium-sized, erect figure, with his Marine Corps overseas "cover" set at a slight tilt on his head, Colonel Maas was every inch an officer. His gleaming black hair had turned quite gray, and he no longer needed a mustache to look "mature." But life was still a dramatic adventure to be greeted with adult wisdom and boyish zest.

On May 21, Colonel Maas arrived by plane at Okinawa Shima in the Ryukyus for special aviation duty with the Commander of the Naval Air Base. Before World War II, Okinawa had been an unfamiliar name to most Americans. Then, and in later decades, they learned that it is part of a chain of islands stretching southward from the main islands of Japan, and is situated only about five hundred miles south of a major city called Hiroshima. Personal involvement is a great geography teacher.

Out in the Pacific, the island-hopping operation had been a "guts and blood" challenge. The Japanese "take-over" had been thorough and devastating, and Tokyo meant it to be permanent.

When General MacArthur escaped from besieged Corregidor early in 1942 and set up headquarters in Melbourne as Supreme Commander of the Allied Forces in the Southwest Pacific, he had very little to work with and Australia was one of the few regions in the area not under Japanese domination.

By the spring of 1945, the Allies had paid a heavy price for their victories, but behind them stretched the battles of the Coral Sea and Midway and bone-weary campaigns on a score of islands with exotic names, where the fighting was gory and desperate and not exotic at all. But the Allies had a job to do, and they were doing it. Even far up in the Aleutian Islands, near Alaska, a violent assault had been launched to dislodge the Japanese from Attu.

As he had promised, General MacArthur returned to the Philippines, landing at Leyte Beach in October 1944, and harassed the enemy right and left until Manila was finally liberated on February 23, 1945. The Allies were closing in on Japan.

By that time, the Fifth Amphibious Corps of the U. S. Marine Corps, with the support of the U. S. Fleet and Air Force, had already reached an historic summit of glory on a small island called Iwo Jima. Almost a month was required to overpower the well-fortified Japanese defenses, and the percentage of American casualties was unusually high—especially for the Marines. When the crashing of bombs had faded and the tumult of battle had dimmed, a picture remained—a magnificent remembrance of an age, a day, a moment when "Uncommon Valor was a Common Virtue."

The vision of grim nobility that climaxed the human sacrifice "on an angry hill" was also captured by Captain T. M. D'Andrea in this verse of "The Ballad of Iwo Jima," which was published in "Leatherneck" magazine in September 1966:

"While those at sea did scan the sky,
To watch the hill where men would die,
Through shot and din of battle's haze,
In sight of God, a flag was raised—
At Iwo."

It could be said that the aggressors of World War II overextended themselves—but only because Allied forces were finally strong enough to stop them.

The story of aggression can be read on a map, a map with blacked-out areas to show how quickly it can spread. There are World War II maps of Europe and North Africa that show the swiftness with which Hitler and Mussolini "moved in for the kill." Maps of Southeast Asia trace the Nipponese tentacles that coiled around Japan's neighbors—and even distant acquaintances—in every direction.

There were three jolly good Maas boys who were doing their part to stop the enemy in World War II. Mel had interested his youngest brother, Bert, in Marine Reserve aviation. Bert, like practically all the Reserves, was on active duty during the war, and he and Mel both served in the South Pacific. The oldest brother, Frank, who had been "tending the store" during World War I, distinguished himself as a Commander in the United States Navy.

A man with a rollicking sense of humor, Frank recalls that the three brothers saw quite a bit of each other during the war. Even though history has proved that the Marines and the Navy can move mountains together, each one hates to admit that the other is really necessary. When asked about the service rivalry in his own family, Frank wrote in one of his delightful letters, "Being the only 'Web Foot' (Sailor) I was given a bad time by the marines, but loved it." It may be noted that Navy Commander Maas capitalized "Web Foot" and "Sailor"—but not "marines."

The three men grasped at their lighthearted moments, knowing full well that war is mainly a deadly serious business. After Bert was wounded and then hospitalized in New Zealand, he was sent home for retirement. By that time, five of the six Maas boys had served their country in the armed forces during periods of critical emergency.

When Colonel Melvin Maas assumed command of the Kadena Airfield, Okinawa Shima, on May 25, 1945, he was replacing an officer whose health had suffered from constant nocturnal visits by the enemy. Air alerts were "routine"—one in the evening, another about midnight, and another early each morning. Sleep came hard for the American defenders.

Coral-reefed Okinawa, with its reddish soil, moderate but humid temperature, and lush vegetation in areas where the rainfall is heavy, had been strongly fortified by the Japanese. The Allies had considered its airfields essential to the launching of major attacks against Japan in the final sweep to victory. The battle for Okinawa turned out to be one of the most furious campaigns of the war, with more than one hundred thousand Japanese and more than twelve thousand Americans killed. There were eighty-two days of fierce combat before organized Japanese resistance was finally quelled on June 21. While American forces were rebuilding the airfields, Japanese air raids continued.

According to one report, "Though actual casualties from enemy air attacks were comparatively light due to the splendid work of our fighters and the heroic part played by ships assigned near picket stations, enemy aircraft succeeded in strafing and bombing both Yontan and Kadena strips frequently." Colonel Maas was entrusted with the monumental job of supervising the enlargement of the Kadena Airfield and keeping it operational under very unfavorable conditions.

In spite of the obvious handicaps, passengers and cargo moved in and out by air, and attacks against the enemy were launched at frequent intervals. Four squadrons of the 2nd Marine Air Wing were based at Kadena.

On July 11, Colonel Maas was appointed commander of Awase Airfield, where he duplicated his previous achievements. While on the Awase assignment, he was wounded during an air raid by enemy bomb fragments. He did not let it bother him much at the time, but the facial wounds would have far-reaching consequences. There was also a leg wound, to accompany the scar he had gotten as a teen-age motorcycle fan.

After all his years of flying airplanes and living dangerously in Congress, Mel Maas won his first Purple Heart for wounds he received on Okinawa at the age of forty-seven.

Colonel Mel Maas ended his term of service at Awase on August 16. Tokyo had surrendered on August 14, after atomic bombs had been dropped on Hiroshima and Nagasaki. It was an event that history would not treat lightly, but it would no longer be necessary to sacrifice hundreds of thousands of additional lives—both Allied and Japanese—in the gigantic invasion campaign that had already been drafted.

Okinawa was one coral-reefed island which would be a major American air and sea base for many years to come. Another generation of Marines would pass that way, looking curiously, but with due respect, at the "sepulchrelike" mounds where native Okinawans bury their beloved ancestors, and viewing all the contrasts between East and West with questioning eyes.

Colonel Maas' splendid record on Okinawa had won him another major honor—the prized Legion of Merit with Combat "V"—for reasons set forth in this handsome citation:

"For exceptionally meritorious conduct in the performance of outstanding services while serving as air base commander at Kadena Airfield, Okinawa Shima, Ryukyus Islands, from 25 May to 11 July 1945, and as air base commander of Awase Airfield, Okinawa, from 11 July to 16 August 1945. Colonel Maas was unusually successful in solving the many varied and complex problems encountered in the organization and operation of Marine air bases. Through the medium of his sound judgment and initiative, he paved the way for the effective utilization of Marine air groups during the assault phase of the Okinawa operation. His exceptional skill and loyal devotion to duty served as an inspiration to all who contributed to the successful operation of Marine air groups against the enemy. He served with distinction throughout and his conduct was at all times in keeping with the highest traditions of the United States Naval Service."

There were bright rows of star-studded service

ribbons on Mel Maas' chest after World War II. He had been awarded the Asiatic-Pacific Campaign Medal with four bronze stars. There was a Victory Medal for him too, and a Presidential Unit Citation for his months of devoted service with the 2nd Marine Air Wing on Okinawa.

Colonel Todd Hays, who has served with the Marine Corps for twenty-eight active years, spoke eloquently of his regard for Melvin Maas during those World War II years and later. "It is natural to associate the term 'esprit de corps' with him," Colonel Hays said. As a young lieutenant in the First Marine Division, Hays did not serve under Colonel Maas, but he was in it from the beginning—serving on Guadalcanal and other "steppingstones" in the South Pacific—and was often able to observe the Marine Colonel from Minnesota in action. He has great feeling for him "as one of the finest gentlemen and greatest officers" it has been his experience to meet.

He recalls that Colonel Maas demonstrated all those high ideals for which the Marine Corps has become famous. "Because he understood excellence and was strongly committed to it, he believed that Marines should be the finest kind of men. He could not tolerate sloppiness or carelessness in procedure —or anything that might reflect unfavorably on the Corps," said Colonel Hays.

Home again in 1945, the book was closed on World War II, but Mel Maas was already reaching out for the next volume in a life that he would never allow to be mediocre.

Chapter Ten

Another Beachhead

When he was relieved of active duty after World War II, Colonel Maas became a Marine Reservist again. He was assigned to Aviation Unit, Ninth Reserve District. He also became a businessman, serving as assistant to the Chairman of the Board of the Sperry Corporation. He had another full life all lined up, especially when his presence was requested again on Capitol Hill during periods of historic consequence in the years ahead.

In 1942, when Marine Reserves had become "Regulars" almost overnight, the Marine Corps Reserve Officers Executive Committee had asked Colonel Maas to "keep a light burning in the window" for the Marine officers who would return to peacetime Reserve status. In 1945, he was summoned from Okinawa by the Commandant of the Marine Corps to supervise the demobilization of about thirty-eight thousand Marine Corps officers. Maas also set about re-establishing the beloved MCROA organization which he had held in "trusteeship" during the war years.

Maas chose a staunch young member of the fraternity, Major William P. McCahill, as his executive director. There were both ladies and gentlemen among the Marine Corps Reserve officers who gave their spirited cooperation to reviving MCROA.

The Commandant of the Marine Corps saluted the Marine Reservists with this postwar commendation: "During World War II, Marine Reserves constituting the bulk of the Marine Corps, had a major share in its wartime achievements. Unfailingly they demonstrated that esprit de corps which is the heritage of all Marines." He looked forward to a splendid era of partnership in which the regulars and reservists would cooperate to achieve "a continuous program of military efficiency."

Mel Maas certainly was not "all tuckered out" from the war. The recent history of "The Marine Corps Reserve" pays tribute to the flurry of energy he brought to the preservation and acceleration of the postwar Marine Reserve. In their office together, he and Colonel Clark W. Thompson "pushed papers, banged desks and fought the memo battles of Marine Corps Headquarters in providing the necessary transition from a wartime to a peacetime Corps in which reservists, finally, would be trained, equipped, and provided first class with the necessary opportunities to serve their country."

The Marine Corps, with a fine sense of respect between the Regular and Reserve organizations, marched ahead into the postwar years in "close formation." In 1946, fifty-two colleges and universities were planning to establish Navy ROTC units, with

Marine officers and enlisted men as instructors. Summer training programs at the Marine base at Quantico were being scheduled for college students who did not attend NROTC colleges but were interested in becoming Marine Corps officers.

All over the country, Marine Reservists were responding with alacrity to the call to give one weekend or several evenings each month, and two weeks each summer, to the peacetime establishment and maintenance of an efficient, vigilant organization. In June 1946, Aviation Reserves flew a total of 2,616 hours. On the ground, a well-balanced system of modern Engineer, Signal, Tank, and AmTrac units was being organized. Reservists were drilling, firing on rifle ranges, handling military vehicles, and generally striving to keep their skills at the peak level of alert readiness that is the hallmark of the Corps.

Far from being out of touch with Congressional activity, Colonel Maas soon answered a call to serve on a Defense Department committee which had been appointed to recommend new legislation relating to the Navy and Marine Corps Reserve. Among other achievements, Colonel Maas is credited with being the guiding spirit behind the 1948 passage of Public Law 810, the only legislative act ever written which provides longevity retirement pay for Reserve officers whose loyalty to duty through the years is deserving of worthy recompense. The first Marine reservist to retire under its provisions was Colonel Harvey L. Miller, who had served in the Regular and Reserve service in both the Navy and Marine Corps for almost forty years.

The senior member of the board, Rear Admiral J. W. Roper, wrote about Colonel Maas' performance on the Defense Department Committee: ". . . His extensive experience as a legislator, as a member of the Marine Corps Reserve and his active service in time of war combined to make his service as a member of the board of the greatest value to the successful completion of the board's work. I consider the report of the board a valuable contribution toward the future effectiveness of the Navy and Marine Corps Reserve, due in large measure to the experience, ability, interest and energy contributed by Colonel Maas."

Even though the House Appropriations Committee and many Congressmen were beaming complimentary benedictions upon the Corps in 1947 and 1948, ominous clouds were again threatening the intrepid Leatherneck organization from the White House and the Pentagon. It was the old familiar story.

Fearing a drastic cut in the regular Corps, Marine Commandant Alexander A. Vandegrift sent out an appeal to former Marines to join the Reserve: "We are calling upon the men whose courage helped smash the enemy at Gaudalcanal, at Tarawa, at Iwo Jima and at Okinawa, to provide an attack force to seize one more beachhead . . ." He did not know that a grave emergency loomed not far ahead when he wrote, "If war should come, the men of the Organized Reserve, trained in the latest tactics and techniques, and armed with the latest weapons, will be ready to join with their comrades of the Fleet Marine force in manning the nation's first line of defense."

Down in the Deep South, another fabulous Marine named "Chesty" Puller was fretting at the top of his lungs. Colonel Puller had wanted ACTIVE duty, but he was assigned to the New Orleans Reserve District instead. General Vandegrift chuckled at the reports that started coming up from New Orleans where Chesty was building up an oversized army of Marine reservists—numbering "a quarter of the organized Marines in the nation." In only a few years, Chesty would have some of those men with him on the other side of the world. On at least one occasion, Puller described the Marine Reserves as an absolute necessity because, ". . . When war comes, there will never be enough professionals to do the job." Burke Davis tells the whole story in his great book, "Marine! The Life of Chesty Puller." Now retired as a Lieutenant General, Chesty Puller has not changed a bit.

Although Chesty Puller and Mel Maas were seldom together, they both believed strongly in Marine Corps readiness, alertness and a high level of discipline. Their loyalty to the Corps was absolute.

Mel Maas had a sensitive ear for any threat to the Marine Corps. He knew that some influential people were actually beginning to ask, "What do we need with a Marine Corps?"—an irreverent question that could be uttered so glibly in peacetime. Debates in Congress indicated that at least one other service felt that the Marines might get too big for their britches.

Colonel Maas, as President of the Marine Corps Reserve Officers Association, fired back an indignant blast in the pages of the MCROA "Word" for November 1947. He wrote, "MCROA never wavered in its battle to assure the integrity of the Marine Corps and to preserve its vital functions by law. Even while others in high places yielded to the pressure from the Administration and Army supporters, MCROA stood fast and held the line. Mandated by the membership, national officers set as the minimum requirements provisions in the legislation that would define our missions and task in the scheme of national security. We insisted that the Marine Corps must by law have the mission of amphibious tactics, that it must retain its own support of Marine Corps aviation. This was in addition to serving aboard vessels of the Navy and guarding Navy property.

"The battle seemed almost hopeless when the Senate yielded to Army pressure and incorporated the weasel-worded provision to the effect that the Marine Corps was not to be disturbed in its relative position—whatever that meant. The national officers of MCROA vigorously carried the fight to the House of Representatives where they were successful in getting their proposals written into law and then accepted in conference with the Senate.

"The twelve Marine members of the House and Senate who helped in this program deserve our gratitude and deepest appreciation for their valiant campaign in Congress on this matter. The 'whip' of the tightly organized Marines in Congress was Major Donald Jackson. Every Marine member of Congress is a member of MCROA. Marines can all go forward now with confidence that the Marine Corps is not going to be abolished nor whittled down by insidious campaigns from inside nor outside the other military services," Maas concluded.

Colonel Maas kept getting letters of commendation. In March 1948, Senator Owen Brewster sent the following letter to Marine Commandant Clifton B. Cates: "This is to inform you that Colonel Melvin J. Maas, USMCR, has made a most able contribution to the United States aviation policy as represented by the Congressional Aviation Policy Board's report. His assistance was of material help in the preparation of the Combat Subcommittee Section."

The Marine Reserves were moving ahead with up-to-the-minute confidence. The Secretary of the Navy's report for the 1948 fiscal year indicated that the Marine Reserve units had been trained in basic military subjects and were supplied with limited amounts of organizational equipment so that it would take approximately one month to mobilize, equip and integrate the organized reserve with the Fleet Marine Force. Units ranged from basic infantry to pilotless aircraft, from ordnance to intelligence. It was noted that a wing staff had been formed under Colonel Melvin J. Maas.

Shortly after the passage of the Reserve Retirement Bill in June 1948, the Marine Colonel from Minnesota led a delegation of two dozen Marine Reservists to the White House and presented President Truman with a gold honorary life membership in the Marine Corps Reserve Officers Association. They were honoring the President who, as a former Army officer, had long advocated Reserve military forces. Mr. Truman had organized the first chapter of the Reserve Officers Association in Kansas City, Missouri.

More and more ladies were becoming a traditional part of Marine Reserve history. The first class of women to graduate from Quantico after World War II took their oath as new lieutenants in 1949. Twelve of the thirty-four were commissioned in the Reserve.

That year was filled with vital developments for MCROA as the benevolent protector of Marine Corps —and Navy—standards. Before 1949 was over, legislation would be introduced by fifty-five members of the House and four in the Senate to guarantee a Marine Corps of adequate size for the future. It would be an uphill fight, with prolonged frustration and some masterful desk-banging all along the way.

Joe Rosenthal's Pulitzer prize-winning picture of five Marines and a Navy corpsman leaning into the wind to raise the American flag on Iwo Jima's Mount Suribachi had caught the imagination of the country. When MCROA held its military conference in Chicago on January 29, 1949, there was a handsome display of decorations from the Iwo Jima float that MCROA had entered in the Inaugural Parade the week before. But tension had been breeding disunity, as the Congressional "sword of Damocles" kept dangling over the Corps. Hopefully, the theme of the meeting was "interservice cooperation and understanding."

Both the Commandant and the Director of Reserve addressed the convention, and there were congratulatory messages from President Truman, Navy Secretary John L. Sullivan, and Defense Secretary James Forrestal to Colonel Mass as National President of MCROA. But the question still remained: If military cuts were made, whose neck would be on the chopping block?

Mel Maas was a man of courage, and he faced the issue squarely when he told the convention: "Never in history was there a greater need for unity, loyalty, and selfless leadership, yet we meet today faced with dissension, backbiting and, frequently, a leadership of selfishness and greed even in our own military forces. Our enemies couldn't, by design, set the stage for their purpose better than we ourselves are doing. What do they see? Still all too much of a mad scramble to either hold blindly to outmoded traditions and weapons, or to greedily reach out and grab control of the weapons, personnel and funds of sister military services, as if the battle were among themselves, instead of a common enemy."

Maas further charged that "bickering, backbiting and sly undercutting, exaggerated claims, slurs, and ill-concealed hostility among too many professional military leaders of all ranks were causing disgust among Americans and gleeful jubilation among our enemies." This, he said, even applied to the attitude of the professional military toward Reserve components. He said that too many Regulars consider Reservists as outsiders, trying to "muscle in" as rank seekers and parasites on their appropriations.

He stated, on the other hand, that too many Reservists have chips on their shoulders and too frequently take the attitude that all Regulars are "brass hats" interested only in holding down the Reserves. He blamed much of the situation upon the "imperfections in the unification law itself" as well as the unyielding attitudes of too many individuals in the military service.

Those who were there summed it up this way: "It was against this backdrop that Maas and the enlightened members of the National Council, together with chapter presidents, urged MCROA to take the lead at the community level in promoting harmony and a spirit of live and let live."

Everyone who loved and admired the bulldogged derring-do of the Leathernecks was plunging to the rescue. Richard Tregaskis, who had observed and reported the awesome exploits of the Marine Corps in the South Pacific during World War II, came out with a rip-roaring feature story, "The Marine Corps Fights For Its Life," in the "Saturday Evening Post" for February 5, 1949. Tregaskis wrote with fierce partisanship of "the never-ending problems which face the Corps, the most grievous being the Marines' current struggle to survive as a fighting unit." This, he noted, was the ninth struggle of that type.

Mr. Tregaskis did not mince words. "The Marines have been the proudest, sharpest American fighting unit for the longest time, the Marine training schools seem capable of inculcating the fiercest esprit de corps—but if the Commandant and his advisers were not alert, they might awake some morning to find that the whole glorious structure had been pulverized by some legislative or administrative blitz."

The opponents of the Marine Corps, Tregaskis hinted darkly, were "mostly Army and Air Force enthusiasts who have long hankered to chop the Marine Corps into nothingness—or worse to a marine—to change it into just another army unit."

Tregaskis spoke of strong "Army pressure" in the committees of Congress, but he noted that the Marine Corps stirred up loyal supporters far and wide, including the Veterans of Foreign Wars, who certainly knew the value of a strong Marine Corps.

Many Navy men were alarmed, too, about the unification bill of 1947. "If the Army and Air Force had so strong a voice in the new setup, the naval air arm like the Marine air arm and the Marines, might be squeezed out of existence."

All the evidence showed that someone was trying to cut the Marine Corps down to size—so that it would never be big enough for "sustained combat."

Later in the spring, a meeting of several hundred Marine Reserve officers was held. Colonel Maas and his colleagues reviewed the previous attempts to absorb or destroy the Marine Corps. Echoing the old proposal of 1929, the most blatant attempt to scuttle the Corps had come from Senator Tydings of Maryland. Army Secretary Kenneth Royal had stated that the Secretary of Defense should be able to transfer the Marine Corps to the Army if he saw fit, and Senator Tydings—as the sponsor of Senate Bill 1269—would make that dastardly development possible.

Was Army General Douglas MacArthur in favor of absorbing the Marine Corps into the Army? He had always wanted Marines with him in his campaigns. According to one reliable source, General MacArthur told Colonel Maas that he approved the merger—because he would like to have some of that inimitable Marine Corps spirit in the Army. Flattery would get MacArthur nowhere with the Marine colonel. Maas could jokingly suggest that the Marine spirit would be diluted if it got mixed up with the Army, but it was a serious controversy all the way through.

At MCROA's October weekend conference in Philadelphia in 1949, Colonel Maas warned that the destruction of the Marine Corps could spell defeat for the United States in the event of another war. "Our history indicates," he said, "that if the Marine Corps is destroyed as a combat organization, we are likely to enter World War III largely with weapons, tactics and techniques developed to fight World War II. They will not be enough to win any future war. The current movement to preserve the Marine Corps as an integrated, well-equipped striking force is basically neither service rivalry nor pride in the Corps, but the deep conviction of people with knowledge that we must have what the Corps can give the nation in order to survive as a democratic nation."

Colonel Maas also emphasized that "the law must provide that the Commandant of the Marine Corps sit with the Joint Chiefs during consideration of amphibious matters and on all other matters affecting the Marine Corps." Since the birth of the Corps, the

Marine Commandant had been "kept in his place." Figuratively, it might be said that he had to listen through a crack in the door when the Joint Chiefs sat. If he were allowed inside, he could be seen but not heard.

While the Great Debate about the fate of the Marine Corps was grinding ahead on Capitol Hill, Soviet-equipped Communist troops from North Korea were moving down into South Korea and the thunder of military conflict again threatened to shake the world. The United Nations had been organized, and it employed its "police powers" to send troops to repel the aggressor from the north.

Right in the middle of the newest crisis, Melvin J. Maas was promoted to Brigadier General in the Marine Reserve on June 1. Early in the 1950's he also was awarded the Armed Forces Reserve Medal and the National Defense Service Medal.

When the call for mobilization came in the United States, the Marines—both Regulars and Reserves—were ready as usual. More than ninety per cent of the officers and enlisted personnel in the Marine Reserve ground forces reported for active duty during the 43-day period following alert orders on July 21, 1950. At the time of the Inchon-Seoul operations in September and October, there were more Marines in the Far East than there had been in the total Fleet Marine Force two and a half months earlier. In less than a year, the Marine Corps tripled its active duty strength, with the Reserve comprising forty-five per cent of the total.

The Marines were in the thick of the most desperate fighting, especially after Soviet aircraft and Chinese Communist troops intervened on the side of North Korea. That the odds were often against the doggedly tenacious Leathernecks is indicated by the fact that they suffered more than 28,000 casualties. The "uncommon valor" of Iwo Jima had been transported into the Korean conflict.

In Congress, the bill to give the Marine Corps the status it deserved was being carried forward by a valiant group of former Marines and Marine reserves, including Senator Paul Douglas, Congressman Mike Mansfield, who had served with Mel Maas in the House during World War II and is now Senate Majority Leader, General Maas and a number of other MCROA leaders.

Outstanding among the MCROA officers with whom Maas continued to work closely was Executive Secretary William P. McCahill, who is now a Colonel in the Marine Reserve. McCahill was the author of "Marine Battle Position 1950," which was featured in "Reserve Officer" magazine early that year. It received the distinction of being inserted in the Congressional Record by Congressman Mansfield who said: "There are many members of Congress who are aware of the attempts being made to reduce the duties and functions of the Marine Corps. We have noted with regret the language and budget estimates as they affect the Corps, but we have also noted with some satisfaction the statement by Secretary of Defense Johnson at his press conference when he unequivocally stated that the Marine Corps would maintain two divisions at reduced strength. This would indicate that more than six Marine battalion landing teams mentioned in the budget message will be considered."

McCahill, in "Battle Position 1950," was in no mood to allow any part of the Corps to be scuttled. "The Marine Reserve today finds himself in a peculiar role," he wrote. "He is on the defensive. After almost making a fetish of the offensive spirit since 1775, the Marine of today is both baffled and belligerent over the role assigned to him in the peace of 1950. The Pacific champ almost has to apologize for being around." He pointed out that "there are brother officers in the civilian reserve who resent the treatment the Corps has been getting in postwar policies almost as much as the Marines themselves. Generally, they are people who either served with or alongside Marines and are familiar with the way a Marine handles a dirty assignment nobody else wants." It was admittedly a biased article, blazing with "esprit de corps."

During that period, Senator Douglas paid tribute to Colonel Maas in a statement that was read into the Congressional Record. In part, he said, "Many organizations with which we must deal here in the Congress of the United States serve various special interests, and their officers are highly salaried. Not only do the officers of MCROA not receive any salaries, but they have no special interests other than those of the Marine Corps and national defense. This . . . is for the benefit of all citizens."

During the continued suspense about the survival

of the Corps, the Military Order of World Wars honored Colonel Maas with its annual Medal of Honor award for rendering the most outstanding service to the national security during 1949. Maas later served with distinction as Commander in Chief of the Military Order of the World Wars.

The 1940's had been both rugged and rewarding for the Marine Corps Reserves who had spent the early part of the decade as Regulars in the South Pacific. In 1948, the "hard-boiled Leathernecks" of the Reserve launched their "Toys for Tots" program, another annual project that has become a tradition. This program has gladdened the hearts of millions of youngsters who might not have Christmas toys—and it is another example of Marine Reserve versatility.

The abrupt necessity for getting another army equipped and trained for overseas combat had produced a tangled mess of human problems. In the fall of 1950, the Pentagon ordered General Maas back to active duty as chairman of a new defense committee of the Reserve Forces Policy Board, to draft an armed forces-reserve reorganization bill. According to the history of "The Marine Corps Reserve," he and the committee were "charged with the responsibility of finding a way to give the civilian soldiers (and their employers) a clearer picture of whether they'd be called to active duty and when." Here was another "Maas-sized challenge." "This means a lot of problems for the Armed Forces," he commented. "No one is going to risk his civilian future to join units, and the only alternative to a decent Reserve is a huge permanent force which the nation cannot afford."

About that time, the General realized that he could no longer find time to serve with the Sperry Company and resigned his position to concentrate on the complicated job of overhauling the Reserve system and making order out of chaos in military-manpower areas.

During the years after World War II, Mel Maas had been on periods of active duty of various kinds for at least a few days of every month. He still felt like a young man, especially when he was flying. No matter what happened to him, he didn't have time to feel old—on the ground or in the air.

Chapter Eleven

Old Marines Don't Fade Away

Although he usually brushed aside any considerations about his own health, General Maas had to face the fact that something serious was happening to both his stomach and his eyes in 1951. He had been troubled by a diabetic condition for a number of years, but it had not slowed him down. If he had a persistent pain in his stomach while he was burdened with the conglomeration of duties on the Reserve Forces Policy Board, he thought it would go away. Richard Tregaskis had been prophetic in his "Saturday Evening Post" article in 1949 when he wrote that quite a few participants were getting ulcers while the Marine Corps was fighting for its life, but Mel Maas didn't think he meant him.

The General's eyesight was still good enough to read a letter that President Truman probably hadn't intended to be circulated so publicly. The President had referred to the Marine Corps as "a police force for the Navy and as having a propaganda machine second only to Stalin's." When the letter ended up in the Congressional Record, it made many Marines and their admirers hopping mad.

That was the first subject that General Maas had on his mind when he addressed the Conference of Chapter Presidents of MCROA on May 19, 1951, in Washington. With typical humor, he started out, "Much has happened since we met a year ago. For one thing, during the year we have been officially proclaimed as the most famous police force in the world, although our propaganda department has been put in question as being only second rate." Speaking seriously, he said that the statement about "the propaganda machine" was "most unfortunate and would be resented by Marines everywhere and would not aid the morale of Marines fighting against Stalin's minions in Korea." He pointed out that the public relations staff of the Marine Corps was relatively small compared to those of the other three services. Instead of loosing a prolonged volley of bitterness, Maas wound up his brief protest by saying almost sadly, "The fundamental tragedy of this ill-timed statement of the President is that it is quite obvious that there is no one available in high places to advise the President as to the mission and functions of the Marine Corps . . ."

The second topic with which he had to deal was a poignant one. For twenty-five years Mel Maas had been the official leader and mentor of the Marine Corps Reserve Officers Association. He had not intended to monopolize the office. He had even threatened on a number of occasions to stay away from the annual meetings unless they elected someone else for a change. But he loved the organization he had helped to found and the people who were part of it, and he knew they often referred to him as "Mr. Marine Corps Reserve." So the years had gone rushing past, and twenty-five of them had fled since he was a curly-headed young Congressman with an Irish glint in his eyes and some splendid ideas about a strong military Reserve in his mind.

Now, when they had finally agreed to accept his resignation because of his many other commitments and the difficulties with his health, he reviewed the panoramic drama of stouthearted men on many an alien shore:

"The Corps, with the help of its Reserves, has written a gloriously new and dramatic chapter in its history and has added a new foreign name to its long list, beginning with Tripoli through Montezuma, Belleau Wood, Guadalcanal and on to Okinawa. Now Korea joins the global record of the Marines. As I make my last report to you, I do so with mixed feeling. Little in my career can ever mean as much to me as MCROA. I step aside without regret and with pride in my association with the finest group of Americans I have ever known . . .

"I believe that in a quarter century of MCROA's existence, the association has left its imprint on the Marine Corps, for we have really developed a fine partnership through these years between the Regulars and the Reserves . . . This relationship has become a pattern for the Reserves of the other military services to aim at. It is just another in the long list of Marine Corps 'firsts.' "

Of Korea, he said, "Just a few years after a war and during the traditional American postwar letdown period, the Marine Reserves were suddenly and most unexpectedly called upon for a gigantic task and quickly. The Marine Corps and its Reserves were equal to the task, to the astonishment and marvel of the world. I think we even surprised ourselves."

Maas pointed out that the missions of the Corps might be considered fulfilled by initial landings and securing of beachheads—but that they had gone far beyond those requirements in every war.

The Marine General had agreed to accept the honor of serving as Board Chairman of MCROA, and they knew that he would always keep in touch—but the wistful gallantry of his farewell words struck an emotional chord: "I hand this challenge and this responsibility on to those who shall be selected today to carry on the direction of the Marine Corps Reserve Officers Association.

"As I say good-by to you as your President, I wish to paraphrase, but slightly change, a recent farewell of a great American. Old Marines, unlike old soldiers, do not die; we don't even fade away; we only step a pace to the rear. So, as an old Marine, I do not 'fade away' from you, but only step back so I may better help from now on by pushing. So, as I step back to the ranks, I assure you that I shall always be in there backing up the younger Marines in the common job of preserving these magnificent United States, by always having a loyal fighting

United States Marine Corps to lead the task force in our preservation."

Of the Truman-Marine controversy, General Richard C. Mangrum said that he doesn't know what the President would have done without the Marines in Korea. Perhaps President Truman was not completely wrong when he spoke of a Marine Corps "propaganda machine," but he forgot to mention that some of the star members of its staff are the man in the street and other volunteer Marine Corps enthusiasts who may never have worn a uniform. There is a special quality about the Marine Corps that stirs the civilian imagination. When there is trouble anywhere, they say, "Send in the Marines!" In an often fickle world, they like the unwavering ring of loyalty in the famous slogan, "Once a Marine, always a Marine!"

Businessmen have responded with boyish excitement when Marine recruiting drives are staged—stringing huge banners across city streets; painting a streetcar red, white and blue and naming it "Marine;" sending up a dirigible to flash the message, "Marine Corps," across the night sky. The Marine Corps does have a public relations department, but the "propaganda machine" gets much of its steam from patriotic American citizens.

While all those Marines were fighting and dying in Korea, the subject of giving the Marine Corps an identity of its own was still hanging fire in Congress and the Pentagon. Nothing in the history of the Marine Corps could be more crucial than some of the reports and bills drafted on its behalf in 1950 and

1951. The most acceptable was Report No. 666, submitted by the House Committee on Armed Services in June 1951, which would put the Commandant on the Joint Chiefs of Staff, fix the active duty enlisted strength at not less than 300,000, and add a safety clause suspending the 400,000 limitation during time of war or national emergency. These and other provisions would assure preservation of the Marine Corps. There were still many months of stalling, anxiety and eloquent oratory before that report would become a legislative reality as Public Law 416.

In working with the Reserve Forces Policy Board, General Maas never tried to influence policy in favor of the Marine Corps. He wanted to develop a fair recruiting and reserve policy for all the services. On one occasion he stated, "At the time of my appointment to the Board, I was informed by the Secretary of Defense that I would be neither a spokesman for the Marine Corps nor responsible to the Marine Corps for my official actions and votes as a member of the Board." Report Number 666, which would determine the fate of the Marine Corps, was another matter.

General Maas' ulcers began to pain him severely while he was testifying before Congress on the Reserve Forces bill that summer, but he was stubbornly reluctant to take time out. He had so many facts at his fingertips, and it was "full steam ahead" if he could only hold out. Between his failing eyesight and those ulcers, it seems impossible that he should have been dynamic. But he was.

Major Gen. Jim Dan Hill (U. S. Army, Retired)

of Madison, Wisconsin, served on the Reserve Forces Policy Board with him. General Hill wrote recently, "I am glad you are writing a biography of my old friend Melvin Maas. He had an instinctive sense for unusual situations and for coping with a crisis. His Congressional career was colorful as was his career as a Marine Corps officer." General Hill continues to be impressed with the coolheaded manner in which young Congressman Maas talked that gunman into throwing his pistol down from the House gallery in 1932.

Mel Maas had the same indomitable spirit in 1951, but he finally had to ship out for Bethesda Naval Hospital on August 28, 1951. As though the ulcers weren't enough punishment, his eyes began to hemorrhage almost immediately. He had always had more than one man's share of courage, but it was torture to realize that the sight in his left eye was failing rapidly and that the other one was deteriorating too. It was believed that the damage had been inflicted during that World War II bombing raid in Okinawa.

Mel Maas didn't take much time to worry about himself, with all that complicated armed forces legislation still hanging fire in Congress. He dictated letters and boomed into the telephone from his hospital room, keeping in touch with committee members and colleagues—blinking through the shadows as though they weren't there. But they were there, and they wouldn't go away.

His wife and daughters and son did not speak in sepulchral voices when they came to visit him in his hospital room. This was a Marine Corps family; its members were not given to maudlin emotionalism. But there was an atmosphere of disbelief. How could this vital, energetic man live without his eyesight? He was always going somewhere at a headlong pace, and now he might not be able to see where he was going—for all the years ahead. They kept hoping and praying for a miracle.

Remembering how the Maas family felt at that time, a point must be made. It doesn't hurt much unless it is happening to you, or to someone close to you.

About two weeks after he had entered the hospital suffering from a severe case of ulcers, a Navy doctor broke the news to him. He did not mince words, and he held out very little hope. "You are a Marine," he told Mel, "and supposed to be able to take it. You are going to be blind; it is quite certain to be permanent." The ulcers, he explained, apparently were only coincidental.

Mel Maas wished that the ulcers had been his most serious difficulty. A fellow could lose a lot of stomach these days and still get along. He suddenly had a mental picture of himself sitting on the sidewalk selling pencils. Would life be worth living? Mel had already learned that he was in the room next to the one from which a despondent former Secretary of Defense, James V. Forrestal, had plunged to his death two years before. Because General Maas had been a Catholic all his life, any contemplations about suicide passed in and out of his mind very quickly.

Colonel Todd Hays, looking back on his own twenty-eight years in the Marine Corps, believes that "the strength of character and self-discipline that is part of all Marine Corps training helped General Maas to face the prospect of blindness with a sense of faith and hope."

It would not be easy. The prospect of being "cut off" from his fellow creatures made him feel dismal. Mel was a sociable person, enjoying spirited communication with thousands of people inside and outside the Marine Corps and Congress. He was an "in" person, whether he was among Marines or members of the more than seventy organizations—local, national and international—to which he belonged during the 1950's.

There were initial hours of searching through the shadows with dismay in that hospital room at Bethesda, especially at night. He had been troubled by insomnia before, but now there was a sensation of trying to keep his head afloat in waves of helplessness. He worried about the financial security of his wife and son. Two of the girls were married, and Patricia was an officer in the Marine Corps, but young Joe was still in school with much of his education still ahead of him. After Mel learned that any officer in the armed forces who is retired for total disability receives a tax-exempt income of seventy-five per cent of the base pay of his retirement grade, he could breathe easier. A year later, when he was retired and advanced to the grade of Major General for having been especially commended in combat, he began drawing approximately $900 a month. As an insurance man who believed in prescribing for himself, he also had a substantial accident-insurance policy.

But there were still many misgivings. After more than thirty years of rushing into active duty, he might end up being the most inactive man in the countryside.

In a feature article in "The Saturday Evening Post" for September 5, 1959, he told Paul F. Healy that he reached the turning point when he summoned up a philosophy that had helped him before. "It is: If you are faced with a problem and can do anything about it, get busy and do it. If your problem is something you can't do anything about, then it is senseless to worry about it."

He began to analyze his problem and experiment, he said. "I still had some sight in my left eye, but I wondered what life would be like when that was gone. One morning I kept my eyes tightly shut as I got out of bed; I went to the bathroom and showered, shaved and brushed my teeth without peeking once. This test brought me profound relief. If I could do that much without any trouble, life couldn't be so bad."

Mel Maas had been acclaimed far and wide as a Marine hero, a fearless Congressman, a valuable adviser to the Defense Department, and a grand fellow with a terrific sense of humor. About the time that he was no longer able to distinguish faces and figures, he really started to become a legend in his own lifetime. The story has been told and retold by everyone who knew him. One day Brig. Gen. Robert Copsey of the Air Force Reserve called his room at Bethesda to ask what he was doing there.

"Bob," General Maas said, "you remember how I always admired beautiful women. Now all women are beautiful." He had turned the corner. He was looking forward, not backward.

His lovely, intuitive wife, Kathy, was determined to help him tear down that wall that might so easily block his way into the future. It was she who brought him some literature describing the rehabilitation course at the Veterans Administration Hospital at Hines, Illinois. But it still seemed fantastic that Mel Maas should need "rehabilitation!"

At home again briefly, the General realized that he had not forgotten how to laugh at himself and life's little foibles. One night at dinner, he recalled, he was groping around his plate with his fork, "But darn if I could spear anything. Seven times I raised that fork to my mouth and drew a blank. I could feel my boy's eyes on me, and there wasn't a sound in the room.

"Then I tried it for the eighth time and the fork was near my mouth when the kid yelled, 'Steady, Pop, you've hit the jackpot!' "

Mel Maas had been rushed to Bethesda Hospital late in August. In November, he was on his way to the Veterans Administration Hospital in Hines, Illinois. He was not just marking time—he was moving forward with much of his old buoyant zest for new horizons. "My religion," he said, "has taught me that if I had the will to take advantage of the compensations, God will give me the strength and confidence."

The General was always on good terms with his religion, but he didn't make a public display of it. His friends often chuckled at the way he would express his approval of brief prayers at meetings. "That was a good prayer," he would say, "nice and short."

In "Please Don't Pity Us Handicapped," Mel Maas described his mental attitude during those months of rehabilitation. "At Hines," he told Paul Healy, "I soon acquired a state of mind which, I am convinced, is one of the most important mental aids to the handicapped. I learned to regard my existence as a continual challenge, full of the excitement of discovery. When I woke up in the morning, I asked myself, 'What new things can I learn today—things that I once thought could be done only with sight?' "

He even overdid it. One day his instructor's car got stuck in the snow, and Mel persuaded him to get out and push while he took the wheel. "I was able to back the car into the middle of the street," he said. "Then I couldn't resist shifting gears and driving forward a short distance." The instructor, who undoubtedly had visions of his sightless pupil driving merrily onward up the street, got back behind the wheel with a distinct sigh of relief.

Mel Maas believed that he had "the finest training in the world at Hines." Russell Williams, the chief of blind rehabilitation at the hospital, was another man who "knew how it felt." He had been blinded by an exploding shell in France in World War II. His staff included instructors in braille and typing, orienters, manual arts therapists, and a counselor.

The orienters were specialists in teaching systematic habit retraining, especially in foot travel. A typical day at the center included orientation and mobility, braille, writing skills, and group recreation. The recreation might consist of bowling, golf or dancing.

One veteran said of the training: "Fear can destroy a man a little at a time. Fear of movement and fear to do ordinary things can injure his mental and physical health. After sixteen weeks at the center, you lose that fear, and this is away above my expectations. The training is more protection for a blind man than a tank is for a soldier."

Mel enjoyed the spirit of camaraderie at Hines, as he and other patients laughed about their fumbling efforts to perform tasks that had seemed so trivial before.

As usual, the Maas capacity for "observation" reached out beyond himself, and he later made these pointed comments:

"During my convalescence at Hines Veterans Hospital, I knew several 'mama's boys' who couldn't learn and wouldn't learn because the mother or wife was overly protective and the blind person was left with the feeling that reading braille, for example, was something too hard; he just could not do it.

"One particular blind young veteran's mother

was overprotective to a point where it interfered with his training. So the staff asked me to see if I could help him with his braille. Well, I tried, but very soon he gave up in exasperation, saying, "That's all right for you, Mel, but me, I am blind." He actually didn't know that I, too, was blind, nor did he care. He was an example of the man who could not learn because his mother was trying to do everything for him. It seemed to me she needed him far more than he needed her, really . . . On the other hand, some families go to the other extreme and expect the newly blind adult to do absolutely everything for himself."

Chapter Twelve

Letter to Marty

The attractive Maas daughters had become young ladies while their father was making Marine Corps history in the South Pacific. The third daughter, Katherine—who is better known as "Sandy"—married Anthony Martino who is now President of Martino Industries in Richmond. When their first son, Marty, was born, the young Martinos were living in Edgemount, Pennsylvania.

The proud grandfather, who was still a patient at Hines, paused to contemplate the miracle of this blessed event. What could he say to his first grandchild that might be of value, of worthwhile significance to little Marty's future?

Out of his vast storehouse of knowledge about people, and their hopes and visions and anxieties, came a letter that is universal in its appeal. Because he recognizes the wealth of inspiration and the richness of the humor in those pages, Marty Martino has generously offered to share his treasure with the readers of this book.

It should be noted that the letter was typewritten. The average sighted person knows that mastering the keyboard of a typewriter can be a fair-sized challenge. Mel Maas began learning to type at Hines, when he was blind. It is remarkable that his train of thought was not "derailed" in some of the long, complicated sentences.

For a letter the size of this one, there were very few errors from striking the wrong keys. In his reasoning and warmth of understanding, Grandfather Maas struck all the right keys when he wrote:

"My dearest Grandson:

"This is my first greeting to you and is written on your dear mother's birthday. I may never 'see' you with ordinary eyesight, but I am sure that you and I will get well acquainted and that I'll see you very well in other ways than my eyes. Eyes, my grandson, are precious, very precious, but they are only one of the ways that enable us to see. In some ways I am fortunate now, since I have had the privilege of seeing with my eyes a good many years and so have a pretty clear set of pictures stored up. Now, when I need to think more clearly than ever before, I am not handicapped by eyesight—I can see from now on with my mind. I find that there are many things that I can see now quite clearly that I couldn't see at all before, or only hazily.

"I hope that it will enable me to do my small part in thereby helping to contribute in some measure to making the world you will have to live in a better place for you. Grandson, it's in quite a mess now, but then it always was! I can remember my grandfather lamenting the state of the world when I was a little boy. So don't be discouraged. Between us, you and I will get it back on the right track. I don't mean just you and I as two individuals, and alone by ourselves. I mean that those of my generation who have not lost faith and who feel the responsibility to try to do something about the mess we have created, with the help of the courageous of your generation, can and will straighten many fundamental errors into a sensible pattern for your generation and those to follow you, so that your children can have a better and saner life.

"Grandson, you have two wonderful parents, and I am sure that you will become as proud of them as they will be of you. You have brought great joy to your father and mother. As the years go by you will bring them increasing happiness.

"You won't have to be a great leader, a famous statesman or business tycoon to accomplish constructive contributions to this cause. You may not become prominent, wealthy, a famous name, but those things are really quite unimportant. What DOES count and really all that does is that in everything that you do DO, you do the very best that you are capable of doing! If your one guide is to do what you are capable of doing and do it with all the capability that is in you, and with the aim of making the maximum contribution to aid in the happiness of those around you, then you will not need to concern yourself with whether you are doing your part, are making your full contribution to life, nor whether you are a success. IF you do your best at all times, then you ARE a success.

"Pay no attention to, and never worry about whether you are considered a success by others. Ignore entirely how your standing compares with others—be concerned only with whether what you do is the very best that it is possible for you to do. Honors, recognition, credit may come or they may not, but they can never mean so much to you as the inner satisfaction of knowing in your own heart that you have done what you knew you must do and that you have done it the very best you possibly could. Honors will turn to ashes in your mouth if you know that they came for accomplishments that did not represent all that you WERE capable of. The inner glow of doing your best whether or not it is publicly recognized, can never be matched by mere acclaim. Fame or wealth for the mere sake of satisfying vanity and possessing power for the sake of being powerful are indeed empty rewards. The only genuine happiness that can come from power, wealth and fame is in using them to make more effective advancements in the causes in which you are dedicated for the betterment of others.

"HAPPINESS DOES NOT COME FROM WHAT YOU GET, BUT ONLY WHAT YOU GIVE!

"And, Grandson, you are being born into the world at a time when you will have the greatest opportunities for accomplishments of the kind that can mean real satisfaction. We who have preceded you have surely left a world of things to be accomplished. You will find a fertile field for any talents you may find that you possess or are capable of developing. There is so much in the world to be done, and you can have so much fun doing your part in it. Sometimes I wish that I were young now, facing the challenges that you will face. However, I probably wouldn't do any better this time than I did so far, and so my hope is that you will make up for my deficiencies by doing your part much better than I did. You will.

"Marty boy, you have a magnificent opportunity ahead of you for a rich, full life of satisfaction, happiness and fun. Pleasure and happiness are not the same thing, but real happiness will give you more genuine pleasure than all the so-called pleasures can.

"One of the greatest and finest sources of happiness is friendships. The way you get real friends is by being a real friend. False friends usually result from false friendships—that is, people who have been cultivated with a motive, usually an expectation that they will in some way be useful to you in advancing you or your interests. Cultivate people for their companionship and the pleasure of the association. Seek people whom you admire and can respect. The satisfaction and happiness from such friends is limitless. Do not limit your choice of friends on the basis of social position, economic status, race, color or creed. If you do, you will be denying yourself many very fine friends from whom you could otherwise enjoy great companionship.

"As one of your grandfathers, I'm not much concerned with what you may decide to do for a career. Whether you become an artist or a lawyer, a banker, follow a military life, go into business, teach or just work is far less important than how you do whatever it is that you do and what satisfaction you get out of it. Should you become a doctor or a bricklayer, just strive to become, not necessarily the best doctor or bricklayer, BUT THE VERY BEST DOCTOR OR BRICKLAYER THAT YOU ARE CAPABLE OF BECOMING.

"Do that and I guarantee you success and happiness in your life. It is happiness that I wish for you above all else. For if you are truly happy it will be because you are making those dear to you happy. Son, there will be unhappiness in your life. There will be sorrows and even tragedies, but my experience is that if you live honestly there will be far more happiness than anything else. There must be the others, if for no other reason than to provide the necessary contrasts to give us an appreciation of the good things. But always remember this, that life will be pretty much what YOU and not what somebody else, makes it for you. You take out what you put in.

"My boy, I'm looking forward to getting acquainted with you and hope it may be soon. It's a little unfair to preach to you like this when you can't defend yourself. And then again you probably will never have to read it. However, in that regard you have nothing on me. Not being able to proofread this, I'm not sure how much of it is even legible.

"One last piece of advice (though you have asked

for none of it). Make your first ambition to not only make your parents happy, but proud of you and you will succeed in making all those close to you both happy and proud of you.

"All my love and tender affection,
"Your Grandfather Maas

"P.S. IF you decide on a military career, I'll give your parents a tip on how to know what service they should prepare you for. They should put a toy ship, airplane and gun in your crib. If you reach for the ship, you will become a navy man. If you reach for the plane—an aviator, if for the gun, an army man, BUT if you reach for the nurse you will become a Marine."

Chapter Thirteen

No Pity, Please

Charlie Jordan remembers that Mel Maas was just as jauntily independent-minded after he became blind as he had been before. Shortly after the General returned from Hines, Charlie saw him marching down the street about ten yards ahead of the person who was supposed to be "guiding" him.

Mel didn't want anyone "fussing" around him. When the subject of a seeing-eye dog came up, he said he already had a wife and three daughters to keep track of him—and they should save the police dogs for people who needed them badly. Mel did not sit around moping. He did not stop living. He began planning for the future.

Because he had been involved in so many projects there, he was familiar with every inch of the house on Dale Drive. He immediately started planning a larger office for himself in the basement. In that comfortable room, with its attractive fireplace, he arranged and rearranged his "office furniture" until he had a U-shaped desk that suited his requirements.

As one idea led to another, he acquired a high-speed chair with casters to zip him from one side of the desk to the other, a telephone, an electric typewriter, a braille transcriber, and albums of recordings that can be borrowed from the Library of Congress.

During the years ahead he would "read" hundreds of books—"talking books." Each month he looked forward to his new talking edition of the "Reader's Digest" to give him six hours of good reading and keep him "up on things."

He "brailled" a long list of telephone numbers and memorized hundreds of them. He dialed numbers as easily as a sighted person—he had pasted a small patch of adhesive tape to the number "five" to use as a guide. He also put tape on the "F" and "J" keys of his typewriter, to get his index fingers started right.

The members of the Maas family marveled at the General's resourcefulness. They tried to cooperate as much as possible, without getting in his way. "Pop" had his own special chairs in several rooms in the house, and they always were kept in the same position. Young Joe Maas, who was already towering over his father as a teen-ager, developed a "sure-fire, if not very delicate" technique for seating his father in unfamiliar chairs. As the older man described it, "He takes hold of my shoulders from in front, pushes me backwards until I reach the chair, then—still holding my shoulders so I don't sit down too soon—commands: 'Now squat.' It never fails."

In his enthusiasm for getting his office ready for

"active duty," Mel Maas sometimes got a bit too frisky. Once, to the consternation of his family, he fell down the basement stairs and skinned his hand severely on the rough stucco wall.

The completion of the office became a "spare-time" project as the General was once more involved in the work he had left behind. Back he went to the Reserve Forces Policy Board to continue setting up a comprehensive Reserve military program.

There was also that important Marine Corps Bill. Report Number 666 would emerge as Public Law 416 after President Truman signed it—and there had been days of anxiety that he might veto it. June 28, 1952, was the day of high suspense. On that Saturday, at noon, President Truman signed the bill into law at the White House in the presence of a former Marine Corps enlisted man named Mike Mansfield. Major Gen. Maas waited in an outer office, while other interested MCROA officers awaited the outcome in MCROA's office not far away. After a five-year tug of war, it was a time for jubilation.

Colonel Tom Wert described Public Law 416 as the "Magna Charta" of the Marine Corps. "Up to this time," he noted, "the Marine Corps could have been dissolved by any President by executive order. This Act, however, gave to the Marine Corps a legal standing and recognition, established a minimum strength of three divisions and three air wings and gave the Commandant membership on the Joint Chiefs of Staff. The part it played in the development and enactment of this legislation has been one of

MCROA's outstanding achievements to date for both corps and country."

This was a triumph for the entire Marine Corps, with special cause for rejoicing "aboard the good ship MCROA." It brought a radiant gleam to the words Mel Maas had written in his own short history of the Marine Corps Reserve Officers Association:

"MCROA through the years, while it has always championed the cause of the reserves, has done so only on the basis of increasing the value of the Marine Corps and at the same time has been the most ardent champion of the Marine Corps itself. We have been able to do many things for the Corps which it was not in a position to do or was actually forbidden to do for itself. The Marine Corps Reserve Officers Association is continuing to march on down the road and adhere doggedly to its original principles.

"Our slogan is 'There will always be a United States as long as there is a United States Marine Corps, and there will always be a United States Marine Corps as long as there is a United States Marine Corps Reserve.' I might add there will always be a United States Marine Corps Reserve as long as there is a United States Marine Corps Reserve Officers Association."

Shortly after the passage of Public Law 416, Melvin Maas became a two-star General, with another hour of destiny soon to follow.

In its March issue in 1956, the "Reader's Digest" featured an article entitled, "One More Career for General Maas." The first few paragraphs vividly described the twilight hour that had caught up with Mel Maas—but had not dimmed his spirit:

"On August 1, 1952, Major Gen. Melvin J. Maas of the U. S. Marine Corps Reserve stood at attention on the parade ground of the historic Marine Barracks in Washington, D. C. A picked ceremonial battalion snapped to 'Present Arms.' The band played the national anthem. In this traditional sundown review the Marine Corps was honoring the two-star General upon his retirement after serving his country in three wars.

"As the last note echoed in the quadrangle, Maas turned to the Marine Commandant, General Lemuel C. Shepherd, and said, 'Sir, the Marines have never looked finer.'

Major Gen. Maas kept right on enjoying parades with boyish enthusiasm. He asked only that someone "cue" him on the proper times to salute and stand at attention. He carried a mental picture of all the parades he had seen before, and especially the evening ceremonies that attract thousands of people to the Marine Barracks at Eighth and Eye Streets S.E., for the traditional evening parades. Here he could view the precision marching with his "inward eye." He could thrill to the spirited rhythm of the drum and bugle corps and feel the same old surges of animation as the Marine Band played majestic martial airs and jolly rakish tunes like "The Irish Washerwoman." He could catch the whispering cadence of the famous "Silent Drill," when no orders are uttered, and only the click and snap of rifles being tossed back and forth with dexterity can be heard. He knew the moment when the flag was lowered into the white-gloved hands of Marines in dress blues and could envision the gleam of trumpets on the ramparts of the barracks as "Taps" ascended to salute a host of twilight memories. And standing erect with pride, he could say, "Well done."

Blindness did not impair General Maas' talents for organization. He wrote the provisions for the Armed Forces Reserve Act of 1952 and the Reserve Officer Personnel Act of 1954, in collaboration with the Armed Forces Reserve Policy Board of the Defense Department, the officers of the Reserve Officers Association, and the Executive Council of MCROA.

On the Reserve Forces Policy Board, Maas concentrated an enormous amount of time and energy on outlining plans that would bring "a common language" to all the reserve units, so they could carry out Defense Department policies and regulations with uniformity. "There are different interpretations of those policies by the services, and by various divisions within a service," he wrote in 1953.

Maas favored arranging for reserve officers to receive military training in foreign countries. He was concerned about officers who neglected their reserve training, and with disability retirement plans that he considered unsatisfactory. Every phase of the reserve program was explored; sometimes he agreed enthusiastically with members of the other armed forces, but he usually wanted to probe deeply into proposals that were submitted. The "human factor" was most important to him, and he was especially opposed to "political type maneuvers" that might undermine the purposes of the Board.

On May 8, 1953, the Secretaries of the Army, Navy, and Air Force were sent copies of the Proposed Directive for Implementation of Section 233 (f), Armed Forces Reserve Act of 1952. It was signed by Melvin J. Maas, Major General, USMCR (Ret.), chairman of the committee that had drafted the new proposal. The directive was primarily concerned with the necessity for effective use of available manpower in time of national emergency or war, the need for maximum fiscal economies in the Armed Services consistent with national security, and the utilization of available Reserve officers to meet increased requirements in time of partial or full mobilization.

The General believed that reservists would perform best if they were permitted to enlist instead of being drafted, and he was especially concerned about the procurement and training of pilots for the Air Reserve Forces.

The morale of the reserves, as individuals, was important to General Maas. In one letter to Board Chairman Charles Buford, he requested that security period medals and ribbons be awarded to all service personnel who had served on active duty after January 25, 1950. "Of the hundreds of thousands of reserves who have been called to active duty," he noted, "only those who served in Korea have any visible effect to show that they have served during this period. This is now a period when we must endeavor to persuade reserves to remain in the reserve voluntarily. One of the things that can be done to appeal to their pride and patriotism is the awarding of such a medal . . ."

It takes awhile to go through General Maas' thick file of Reserve Forces Policy material. There are dozens of examples of his well-rounded thoughtfulness. For instance, when Charles H. Buford relinquished office as Chairman of the Reserve Forces Policy Board, he commended General Maas in a letter to the Commandant of the Marine Corps. After receiving a copy of that letter from Commandant Shepherd, General Maas wrote to tell "Charlie" Buford that he was "deeply grateful for his kind and generous remarks." He also wrote to thank the Commandant for sending him a copy of Buford's letter.

All the purposeful liveliness in Mel Maas' character is apparent in those letters. Abruptly, in the middle of the file, the enthralled researcher is jolted by a poignant reminder of his condition. There is a braille marker attached to the 1954 list of members of The Reserve Forces Policy Board. It is easy to forget that those letters originated with a man whose eyes could see nothing but darkness.

General Maas also served on the Marine Corps Promotion Board during that period. He was both gracious and aggressive about recommending qualified officers for promotion.

On December 10, 1954, the retired Marine Corps General reached another milestone in his life when he received the following letter from Secretary of Defense Charles E. Wilson: "Upon the occasion of the expiration of your term of office as a member of the Reserve Forces Policy Board, I wish to commend you for your outstanding contribution to the work of the Board and to the national interest. We all recognize that you are one of the charter members of this Board with over four years of valuable service to this Department . . .

"The important part which you have played in the Board's achievements since its inception is acknowledged with deep apreciation. I am very desirous of retaining your experience during the current situation concerning the Reserve Program . . ."

There were other laudatory letters of that type from government officials and top-ranking military officers, most of them requesting appointments for further consultation about the Reserve Forces project on which General Maas had become an authority. General Maas expressed his appreciation and assured them that he would be available. "The contribution that can be made by the proper reserve force to our national security has been close to my heart for many years and always will be," he wrote.

On August 17, 1955, after President Eisenhower had signed the Reserve Forces Act of 1955 into law, General Maas was among those who received letters of appreciation from Assistant Secretary of Defense Carter L. Burgess. The victory had been achieved at last, but Mel Maas kept his interest high during the formative stage as the new Ready Reserve and

Standby Reserve programs were put into action for all the services.

In August 1966, when "Leatherneck" magazine saluted the Marine Reserve Establishment on its fifty years of historic survival, it noted that the Marine Corps Reserve had reached "the status of a division/wing team. It can mobilize and be prepared to mount out for combat in 20 days."

Of the program on which General Maas and the other members of the Armed Forces Policy Board had labored so persistently, "Leatherneck" wrote:

"One of the greatest assets to the Organized Reserve training program—the factor which makes today's state of readiness possible—was the establishment of the Six Months Active Reserve Program which began in 1955. This is the program which permits a young man to take Regular Marine training syllabus for six months, then serve the remainder of his six years' obligated service in a hometown Reserve unit. From this six months' active duty program, Reserve units keep their ranks filled with trained and partially trained young enlisted men. Officers enter hometown units after a minimum of two years' active duty.

"The six months' active training is enough time for a man to complete recruit training, take individual combat training, and learn the fundamentals of his Military Occupational Specialty. In many cases, especially when a man is assigned to learn one of the harder skills such as aviation electronics or auto mechanics, he can remain on active duty longer than six months in order to finish formal school training. Even after he has finished his six months' training, a man may return to active duty for specific training under the Extended Training Program."

General Maas continued to be interested in the perpetuation of an alert, well-informed Reserve Forces Policy Board.

The Six Months Active Duty Reserve Program "struck close to home" in the Maas household. Young Melvin Jr.—Joe—took time out from school to serve his six months of active duty at Parris Island and Le Jeune, and he continued with his six years of Marine Corps Reserve service when he was a student at the University of Maryland.

The blind General's years of usefulness were far from over, because his eagerness to learn and to serve continued undiminished. He was the same man—with his abilities slightly rearranged. That was a point he would often make in the years to come. An individual's other faculties will be sharpened if some part of the human machinery "goes on the blink." Mel's memory became more fabulous than it had ever been, as though everything he heard was engraved on that blank screen in front of his eyes. Marine Colonel Daniel Omer, a former Minnesotan who has been stationed in Washington, recently spoke with awe of Mel Maas' ability to recognize his voice. Both of them attended Minnesota Chamber of Commerce meetings in Washington. Even though six months had elapsed, Mel Maas would greet Dan Omer by name as soon as he heard his voice.

Since Maas had become acquainted with thousands of people before he lost his sight, he was not always that adept at picking voices out of a crowd. Blind people, he said on one occasion, are "put on the spot" by people who come up to them and whoop, "You know who I am, but tell me anyway!"

When one persistent fellow, whom he hadn't seen for ten years, insisted on playing the "name-guessing game" at length in public, Mel became so irritated that he finally exploded, "I don't give a d - - - who you are!" His outburst did nothing to revive the friendship, but it did indicate that blind persons are often dismayed when friends grab them and insist playfully, "Guess who this is." With an audience around, it is especially embarrassing.

The considerate thing to do, according to Mel Maas and other blind people, is to mention your name at once and add some other identifying comments.

As he wound up his years as an influential figure in Congress, Mel Maas made a remark that has become classic. When he was testifying on the Reserve Bill, a colleague said, "You are the first general in American history to serve without sight."

"Oh, no," Mel answered with a chuckle, "just the first to admit it."

Chapter Fourteen

The New Career

Melvin Maas had retired from the Marine Corps and his term of service on the Armed Forces Reserve Policy Board was officially ended, but he still had more places to go and more things to do than most people with two good eyes. He continued to be interested in the work of Congress, the reserves, and the good fellowship of all the people whose company he enjoyed. But he only tried to give his attention to about twenty of the organizations to which he belonged—at one time.

When General Maas "saw" the need for a new organization somewhere, he was ready to help out. Joe Bartlett, the reading clerk in the House, has a store of priceless memories about the Congressional Marines Breakfast Group which, since 1953, was one of General Maas' favorite associations.

Joe Bartlett immediately fits into the category of "nice guys." In his office, high up in the Capitol, a motto on his filing cabinet proclaims: "He Who Laughs — Lasts." Joe's friendship with Mel Maas dates back to the prewar years when the older man was a Congressman and Joe was a House page.

Along came World War II, bringing kaleidoscopic changes in everyone's life. When Colonel Melvin J. Maas came flying back from the South Pacific during the war, he found his young friend, Pfc. Bartlett, working as a transportation clerk in Marine Headquarters in San Francisco—the official base of "The Department of the Pacific" at that time. The Colonel rushed over to the Pfc. and made such a fuss over him that some of the other military personnel raised their eyebrows. "He was never a stuffed shirt about rank," Joe recalls with a fond grin.

Joe credits Mel Maas with getting him promoted to "noncom" after the war. The Meritorius Noncommissioned Officers program had been adopted, and Bartlett had passed the qualification tests. When Colonel Maas learned that the promotion was being held up because no quota had been established, he went straight to Acting Commandant Lieut. Gen. Merwin H. Silverthorn.

"Why isn't there a quota for that program?" he wanted to know. "I have a man who qualifies."

"All right," replied the General. "We'll set up a quota of ONE!"

Joe soon learned through official channels that he had become a noncommissioned officer in the Marine Reserve. He didn't learn it from Mel Maas. When Mel did special things for people, he never came around afterward to collect the credit.

He could have taken credit, so many times, but he

always wanted to divide it up—to make other people bask in the glow of achievement with him. There was the Marine Breakfast Group, composed mainly of members of Congress and Capitol Hill officers who had served with the United States Marine Corps. Both General Maas and Joe Bartlett are listed as charter members. To hear Joe tell it, the group flourished because of the General's support. Other people have heard the General say that the Breakfast Group wouldn't have been a success without Joe Bartlett's talents for organization. Both Commandant Wallace Greene and Lieut. Col. Patricia Maas agree that Joe Bartlett certainly "caught the torch."

One of the members was Jimmy Roosevelt, a fellow-Marine who had served with Maas in the South Pacific. Although Maas had indulged in some strong differences of opinion with President Roosevelt, he enjoyed a firm friendship with his son, Congressman James Roosevelt from California.

The Breakfast Group meetings are informal and sociable, with no dues or permanent officers, and so the group survives. Joe likes to remember the times when he drove six miles out of his way, to pick Mel up and take him to the monthly reunions—for the sheer pleasure of those early morning conversations. Joe winces as he recalls the reeking fumes of Mel's cigars before breakfast, defiling the fresh morning air. "But he knew exactly where the ash tray was, and he never missed it." Here was the most "fabulous" aspect of those trips: "The General kept discussing landmarks and areas of the city as we drove past them. He knew the route and what was going on, even though he couldn't see anything. It was fantastic!" Joe said.

Washington had been home to the General for a great many years. After he lost his eyesight, he would say, "I can do everything except drive in Washington traffic—and I don't know who the hell wants to do that anyway!"

Joe did not consider the General a "restless conversationalist." He would settle back and make his companions feel relaxed and in high good humor. But there was always a sense of "drive" to him. He was a man who would rather run one mile than plod dully along for a hundred.

Before and after he lost his sight, General Maas made an unforgettable impact on Joe Bartlett. Joe has trouble recalling anything that wasn't good and decent about him. Even when he disagreed with people, most of them kept thinking of Mel Maas as "a great guy."

As sick as he sometimes was, with ulcers and diabetes and a variety of ailments, the General often disregarded his doctor's orders because he felt he should keep speaking engagements. "I promised," he would tell Joe Bartlett. "They are expecting me."

The General was more interested in "bucking up" the health of other people. When General Alexander A. Vandegrift, the hero of Guadalcanal, was desperately sick in the hospital, General Maas dropped in to see his old friend. Knowing that General Vandegrift was in a state of despair about his health, he launched on a rousing pep talk. "You can't give up," he said. "You've got to write a book about the South Pacific campaign—you owe it to the Marines who served with you! Why, you can tell the story into a tape recorder, right there in bed." General Vandegrift did write that book.

It is still incomprehensible to Joe Bartlett that General Melvin Maas, a man who was forging ahead so vibrantly at the age of fifty-three, should have been stricken with blindness. He had fought his battle and made his peace with his affliction at Hines, but Joe said there were still some periods of soul-searching after he got back. He sometimes wondered if he had been fair to himself and his family when he went into politics, if it might not have been better to continue with his business career. His children remember that he took enormous pride in his financial talents. "Of course, he could have been a millionaire!" Joe Bartlett agreed.

Once Mel ended a "soul-searching soliloquy" with a hearty laugh as he recalled that he had been driving a Cadillac when he entered Congress and was driving a Chevrolet when he left. All in all, service in the Halls of Congress seemed more important to him than accumulating a handsome estate. It was something that could not be measured in terms of money.

The great tragedy in his life, perhaps, was the knowledge that he could never again fly an airplane. It had been his life, his joy, his great delight. He understood aircraft and the wonderful things they could accomplish — in world travel and trade, in peace and war. To say nothing of the extraordinary antics they could perform. When another Joe—Mel's son—was old enough to get around the country, he learned that his father had already become a "living legend on wings." "After one fellow found out that Mel Maas was my father," Joe said, "he told me he had seen 'Pop' leading his aviation squadron under the high bridge at Indianapolis!" Needless to say, they were not afoot.

But Mel Maas had flown for all those years without an accident. When he performed spectacular feats, he must have figured his margin of safety carefully.

The story of Mel's last effort to handle a plane in flight has been celebrated in print and in the spoken word. As Joe Bartlett put it, "He just had to get his hands on the controls of a plane, even on the way back from Hines!" He was riding back to Washington on a transport plane, and he took the liberty of asking the pilot to let him sit in his seat to get the "feel" of the familiar controls again. The pilot may have been apprehensive about a man who would be "flying blind," but he could detect the wistful note in the General's voice.

Mel was feeling exultantly blissful until the pilot told him politely that he had just made a ninety-degree turn off course. When he tried to "compensate," the pilot said he was doing fine—except that he had slightly overdone the correction.

General Maas started talking to some young Marines when he went back to the cabin, and he couldn't resist confiding that they had just been piloted by "the blindest pilot in the business." When one of them blurted out that he had been doing swell—especially on that 360-degree turn—Mel realized that he must have been flying in circles. He decided, right then, that his piloting days were over.

Although he was unable to see, no one doubted his ability to think, and General Maas had some substantial offers from business firms that would have valued his services in 1953. He might still have become a millionaire, but perhaps his life had already started up a new high road, back in 1947, when President Truman appointed him to serve on his National Employ the Physically Handicapped Week Committee. Maas thought he had been chosen to represent the military at that time. Even though he was deeply interested in the problems of disabled veterans who needed rehabilitation and employment, the idea that he would ever be among the "physically handicapped" was remote from his mind.

By December 1953, when President Dwight D. Eisenhower asked General Maas to serve as vice chairman, the original 1946 committee had gone through a process of evolution. The Citizens' Cooperating Committee of the Retraining and Reemployment Administration was eliminated when its government sponsoring agency went out of existence in early 1947. For a short time, a private organization tried to fill the breach. In the fall of 1947, the vitally important movement was at last given stature by a Presidential mandate that would eventually arouse "grassroots" interest in a year-round employ-the-handicapped program. It took two more years for

Congress to vote necessary funds to further the work of committee volunteer citizens under the direction of a small staff in 1949.

When Maas succeeded Earl H. Gammons, vice president of the Columbia Broadcasting System, as vice chairman of the President's committee, he issued this statement in December 1953:

"I am very appreciative of the President's appointment and the opportunity for enlarged service in the field of obtaining employment for the physically handicapped. I am intensely interested in this work both from a standpoint of being the finest type of example of democracy in action and also meeting a most essential need for the nation itself for increased national production.

"Democracy and Western civilization are based on the concept of the dignity of the individual. Nothing so contributes to the dignity and self-respect of an individual as being able to take his full place in the social and economic life of the community. To the seriously physically handicapped this has always been a problem.

"Since we are facing a potentially hostile segment of the world with vastly greater manpower available than we have, we must make every man and woman count to the maximum. This means that every man and woman capable of rehabilitation for useful work must be so rehabilitated and adjusted into the working force of the nation. I foresee every increased success in this endeavor under the guidance and leadership of The President's Committee on

Employment of the Physically Handicapped." The name had been shortened to emphasize the year-round mission.

A Marine, the saying goes, is expected to be both versatile and resourceful, and General Maas had demonstrated those abilities in a variety of areas. He had been a "Semper Fidelis" man wherever he had served. The President's Committee would be a change of pace from his military activities. In his uneasiness and anxiety about the unsettled condition of the world, Maas had sometimes appeared to be the most vociferous saber-rattler in Congress. The fact that he was beloved by political intimates of both parties indicates the widespread respect for his opinions. Even the strongest pacifists sometimes found themselves sharing the realistic doubts of the Minnesota statesman.

His arguments were not always popular. It was assumed that World War I would make the world "safe for democracy." During the 1920's and 1930's, the United States and most of the nations of Europe were committed to an ideal of peace. They wanted no more bloody battlefields, no more tragic sacrifices of their fine young men. But, in at least two nations of the world, a whole generation of German and Japanese youth was being trained and educated to the irrational belief that death in war could be glorious—that dying for an aggressive "fatherland" was much more noble than remaining alive.

No matter how badly most of the world wanted peace, Mel Maas saw that all of human nature would not be changed everywhere overnight. The United

States must remain strong, he believed, through periods of cold and hot confrontation, until every nation in the world stopped preaching doctrines of hatred and brainwashing its young people to fight wars of aggression.

In 1945, when he talked about Communist China as a threat to world peace, it was as though he feared that the leaders of the huge mainland Chinese nation might someday speak lightly of atomic warfare and of sacrificing hundreds of millions of Chinese lives in the burst of retaliation that would surely follow. He knew that the world had not yet progressed through its age of illogical contradictions into an era of civilized faith and hope for all of humanity. He seemed to be saying in effect, "We have heard the relentless crunch of marching feet and the slogans of hatred too many times. We must never be caught off balance."

In her recollections of Colonel Maas' conversation in 1945, Suzanne Steiner said that the remembrance of that evening was a "consolation" two decades later. The Steiners' 21-year-old Marine Corps son was on his way to Southeast Asia. "Thanks to him I know why our son has to go!" she declared.

During those years of national defense activity, General Maas had been concerned with teaching Americans to sleep with one eye open in a sometimes hostile world. He was not a lover of war, but he was dedicated to the cause of adequate preparedness. In 1954 he became a teacher of a different sort. All the warmth of his good heart, which had been so evident in that letter to Marty, responded to the new call to active duty. On April 13, he succeeded Vice Admiral Ross T. McIntire as Chairman of the President's Committee on Employment of the Physically Handicapped.

Mel Maas had known President Eisenhower as a young Army officer and later as a five-star general. Quite a few years before, when Major Eisenhower had been stationed at a desk outside the offices of General Douglas MacArthur and Assistant Secretary of War Hanford McNider, Congressman Maas would be among the visitors who arrived to attend conferences. Most of the Congressmen who came to see "the top echelon men" treated Major Eisenhower like a receptionist, but "Ike" remembered that Congressman Maas always stopped to exchange some friendly remarks with him.

It was a tremendous honor to be appointed Chairman of the President's Committee on Employment of the Physically Handicapped, even though there was no salary for that job. This, too, was typical of Mel Maas.

The committee had grown under Admiral McIntire, and it would continue to expand under General Maas' exuberant, dedicated chairmanship. Maas immediately revealed his familiarity with the "humanitarian battlefield" that would be his new base of operations. He admonished one of his audiences to help prove to the Asian and African that "we welcome him with open arms, we treat him as an equal and respect his dignity; then we can have a real partnership in this world where there no longer is a question of color or race or creed or physical condition of the individual."

When he began his new career, Mel had an office on the first floor of the Department of Labor, and he could find his way to it without any difficulty—under ordinary circumstances. Joe Bartlett said that other friends enjoyed giving the General a "lift" after he became blind. On one unforgettable morning, Marine Commandant R. M. Pate picked him up and drove him along Constitution Avenue—"where all those monumental white buildings look the same"—to the front of what was supposed to be the Department of Labor Building.

Independent as usual, the General got out of the car, marched up the steps, and walked the usual number of paces down the hall into what was supposed to be his office. The desk was in the right place, so he sat down as usual. By and by, someone with an unfamiliar voice came along and gently broke the news to him that he was in the Internal Revenue Building, sitting at someone else's desk.

A driver was called to deliver him safely to the Labor Building. Whenever Mel told that story, he howled with laughter. He thought it was a great joke on Commandant Pate.

Chapter Fifteen

The Miracle

There were people close to Mel Maas who had prayed that he would not lose his eyesight. It has been said that God always answers prayers—either with a "yes" or a "no." When he answered "no" to the petitions for Mel's eyesight, the years ahead would reveal that this might have been by far the greater miracle.

On his first trip abroad for the President's Committee, General Maas started to become a legend as a "lone" traveler. After attending an international veterans' rehabilitation conference at The Hague, he flew on to Paris for some military conversation with his boyhood friend, General Alfred Gruenther, who was then Supreme Commander of NATO. After they talked for awhile, it occurred to General Gruenther to ask, "Who is with you, Mel?"

He was astonished to hear Mel answer, "No one." General Maas hastened to explain that he had been provided with an escort on his first trip after he became blind. "But," he added, "the escort became so airsick that I had to take care of him. So I decided just to take care of myself after that!"

If no one was meeting him at the airport when he was traveling in the United States during those years, he would ask a skycap to get him a taxi. Priding himself on his ability to get around, he would progress from skycap to taxi driver to bellhop in an orderly fashion. Often his picture appeared in papers, debarking from a plane with a jaunty air, his cigar clamped in his mouth—minus dark glasses and police dog. As far as possible, he made every effort not to "look" blind.

When he assumed the chairmanship in 1954, General Maas paid tribute to the work done by Admiral McIntire as chairman since the inception of the committee in the fall of 1947, saying, "The climate of public opinion which is today so favorable to increased employment opportunities for the physically handicapped is due in large part to the leadership of Admiral McIntire. Through his devoted work much has been accomplished and the job ahead is a great challenge."

The President's Committee had made remarkable gains, and it was not destined to remain static under the imaginative direction of Major Gen. Maas. When he was not an originator, he was a lusty builder on foundations that had already been laid.

His qualifications as an organizer, a leader, and a student of human nature were perfect. Because he had fought the good fight with his own disability and had emerged victorious, he could show others that they could rise above their handicaps. Of even greater significance, he could demonstrate to prospective employers that blindness had not kept him from being an extremely valuable citizen. He would have been an asset to any business. By "selling himself," he was selling an idea—that a handicapped person is employable, whether it's a man named Melvin Maas or a girl named Jane Doe.

Rehabilitation and job placement are in the hands of a variety of other offices and agencies, and the President's Committee is not authorized to provide them. Rather, its purpose is to stimulate and maintain a high degree of constructive awareness of the handicapped as welcome, useful members of the human family. Let's put it this way. Today you are rushing about on your normal routine. Tonight you are in an automobile accident that causes the loss of one of your arms or legs. You will be sickened by the shock of it for awhile—but are you really a different person? In almost too simplified terms, it is the purpose of the President's Committee on Employment of the Handicapped to tell the world that you are not "different."

Perhaps you might be stricken by a disabling illness, as Ann Adams was. Ann, a polio patient, was an artist before her illness. Refusing to feel that she was any less an artist, she trained herself to draw exquisite sketches for note paper—by holding a pencil between her teeth. The only thing "different" about her is her phenomenal gallantry.

Back in the dark ages of civilization, people with

disabilities were almost completely rejected by society. As social consciences were awakened to their plight, they became "limbo personalities," deserving of a bit of charity and much more pity than they wanted.

With the publication of "The Saturday Evening Post" article, "Don't Pity Us Handicapped," Mel Maas inspired more Americans to examine their own attitudes. Did they feel awkward around disabled people? Was it pity or prejudice? That article convinced them that it would be great sport, and a thrill too, to know a man like Mel Maas. How could anyone pity so wise and gallant a human being? He was so far ahead of most "sighted" people.

The handicapped, said Mel Maas, want training and jobs—not pity or prejudice. They want to demonstrate that they can function and contribute as willingly as people who are "whole."

You will find some of the most delightfully healthy-minded people in the world among Mel Maas' colleagues, on the seventh floor of the Labor Building. Bernard Posner, the Deputy Executive Director of the President's Committee, has a very sunny disposition. "Don't you ever get depressed," I asked Bernie, "when you need to be concerned about so many disabled people, day after day?"

True to the philosophy of Mel Maas, he said, "You don't see the disabilities. You see the whole person."

Congress passed a law in 1954 to accelerate the rehabilitation of the disabled. From a modest beginning less than ten years before, General Maas sought to extend the gigantic pattern of involvement in the human rights crusade for the handicapped. There was a wealth of printed evidence depicting the zeal of his predecessors.

Monthly issues of a slim publication called "Performance" have told the story of the rehabilitation and employment of the handicapped ever since 1950. The cover picture, in July 1950, showed a smiling, curly-headed young man who incidentally happened to be handicapped. Albert Wenger of Minneapolis had lost both forearms and both legs below the knees, but he was shown working at a factory job after his home state provided rehabilitation services.

"Performance" now adds up to many bound volumes filled with revelations about the ability of handicapped people to achieve or to return to first-class citizenship.

In the introduction to that first issue of "Performance," Secretary of Labor Maurice Tobin wrote, "Through this type of publication . . . we hope to bring about a better understanding of the real abilities of the physically impaired and to provide a medium for the exchange of ideas and information that will be of value in furthering employment opportunities for our physically impaired citizens."

With such an abundance of vivid "thumbnail" sketches in "Performance" and other President's Committee publications, it is difficult to select just a few to show what was happening to some of the disabled heroes of World War II and Korea. There was Joseph F. Lathan, a Navy veteran who had lost a hand, but was not acting disabled. By using a twin-claw device and his one good hand, he was assembling and disassembling highly specialized pieces of ordnance equipment with as great skill as most men achieve with two hands.

The paragraph about Ralph E. Forey is as good as a "sermon." "Wounded by German bazooka fire, Forey lost his left eye and received chest and stomach wounds. Guidance tests revealed the same mechanical aptitude that he had before the war. He finds that his work is in no way impeded by his disability. His latest efficiency rating was 'very good.'"

The fighting in Germany was almost over when a mortar shell ripped off one of Gene Hinkle's legs, and the other one had to be amputated. After twenty-eight major operations, he went home to Fayette County, Kentucky, where the Fayette County Police Department hired him as a dispatcher—thus relieving another officer for duty. His job demands lightning decisions—sending prowl cars to trouble spots, keeping contact with the entire county police force, sandwiching in all the record-keeping for the department. He became a valuable man in an important spot.

Although blinded in combat during World War II, George Lester became a skilled assembler of venetian blinds in the shop where he was receiving vocational retraining under Veterans Administration sponsorship. His employers said that he worked as accurately and more rapidly than most men with normal sight.

Officials of Columbia Steel, a subsidiary of the U. S. Steel Corporation, stated in an early issue of "Performance" that, "Handicapped workers receive no special consideration since they are placed on jobs that they can do as well or better than their able-bodied co-workers." It was further noted that "many of them are superior workers, probably because they make a determined effort to prove to themselves and to the company that they are fully capable of handling their jobs satisfactorily and safely."

"Performance" has often saluted the resourcefully self-employed. There was William Austin Betterly, president of the Fibrous-Glass Insulation Company, who had pawned his wristwatch to buy Christmas dinner for his wife and daughter in 1950. Two years later, his small, bustling factory, which had just completed 30,000 parachute packs for the Air Force without a single rejection, was causing a "mild uproar" in manufacturing circles. "Not only did the company, manned entirely by physically handicapped workers, complete the Air Force order in record time, but it turned back to the Government $6,000 of unused funds on its contract." All of the men in the factory were disabled veterans—"the guys nobody wanted," and William Betterly included himself in that category — but representatives of other firms were soon touring his plant to find out how his small company was managing to do everything better.

In telling the story of the handicapped, "Performance" also devotes much attention to people who were born with physical defects and who form a large number of the hundreds of thousands of disabled. One of them was Henry Viscardi Jr., who was "an uncommon child and an uncommon man." He described himself as "a crippled child, horribly deformed," and he remembered asking his mother why this should be.

"She told me that when it was time for another crippled child to be born, the Lord and his councilors held a meeting to decide where it should be sent, and the Lord said, 'I think the Viscardis would be a good family for a crippled boy.' " Viscardi thought that a great country like America should be "a good family" for the crippled and disabled. In his life of dedication to the disabled, he wrote with his head and spirit high:

"I do not choose to be a common man. It is my right to be uncommon—if I can. I seek opportunity—not security. I do not wish to be a 'kept' citizen, humbled and dulled by having the state look after me. I want to take the calculated risk; to dream and to build, to fail and to succeed. I refuse to barter incentive for a dole. I prefer the challenges of life to the guaranteed existence; the thrill of fulfillment to the stale calm of Utopia. I will not trade freedom for beneficence nor my dignity for a handout. I will never cower before any master nor bend to any threat: It is my heritage to stand erect, proud and unafraid; to think and act for myself, to enjoy the benefit of my creations and to face the world boldly and say, 'This I have done.' "

In Los Angeles County's United Cerebral Palsy Industrial Production Workshop, "C.P." had already come to stand for "can produce" by 1955. Many cerebral palsied workers were on the road to economic independence. They had acquired practical training and skills that would qualify them for employment in private industry. In the workshop, they had filled contracts and earned wages as they learned.

There have been close ties between the President's Committee and Goodwill Industries, Inc., which provides training, employment and rehabilitation services for thousands of handicapped people annually. "Goodwill" stories have often been featured in "Performance." One group of pictures showed disabled workers at Goodwill Industries in Washington, D. C., busily reconditioning toys at Christmas time.

In 1955, President Eisenhower gave additional recognition to the President's Committee on Employment of the Physically Handicapped by establishing an advisory council for it and assigning it coordinating functions among different agencies working in the rehabilitation field with respect to job opportunities. Associate members of PC include all the Cabinet Members, the Administrator of Veterans Affairs, the Chairman of the Civil Service Commission, the Director of the Office of Emergency Planning, and the Administrator of the General Services Administration.

Substantial progress in job placement of the handicapped had been achieved through the Labor Department's Bureau of Employment Security, and the support of many labor-management and employer-community leaders had been enlisted. The

Department of Health, Education and Welfare had been cooperating actively in its related fields. But, when Mel Maas moved to the chairman's desk of the President's Committee, there was—and there still is—much to be done. This applies as much to employers as to disabled workers seeking jobs, as Mel Maas often pointed out. Getting them together has been the problem from the beginning.

General Maas was involved in a heavy traveling schedule almost immediately. He got off to a "flying start" and his colleagues say that it got so all the stewardesses were calling him by name.

When he was in his office between trips, he got a fantastic amount of correspondence out of the way in short order. Dorothy Dunnigan, who became his secretary, considered him "a phenomenal worker," and she should know. He would dictate a shattering avalanche of letters, hour after hour.

Mel still loved his cigars, and he would fill the room with billowing clouds of smoke. Dottie recalls his first day in the office, when he sat down at his desk, smoked four cigars and dictated twenty-eight letters—all in three hours. The door was closed, and Dottie was relieved when someone opened it to look in. She made gasping motions, and her co-worker caught the hint and left the door open so some of the smoke could escape. When the dictating session was over that day, she whispered to someone that she certainly had needed an Airwick. The next day General Maas marched in and gallantly presented her with a gift package. Inside was a bottle of Airwick!

Did Mel Maas have trouble finding someone to light his cigars? If that had been necessary, he probably would have had to quit. Always independent and resourceful, he taught himself to put on a fascinating performance—sticking a cigar between his teeth and running a match gently along the bottom of it. When he felt the match touching the tip of the cigar, he rubbed a matchbox against both. Presto—the cigar was lighted, and he could puff to his heart's content, no matter what it did to the people around him.

In his new "mobilization program" against prejudice and indifference, history was duplicating itself for General Maas. Major William P. McCahill had been Maas' MCROA Executive Secretary. Bill McCahill was already officiating as Executive Secretary of the President's Committee when General Maas agreed to serve as chairman. Bill and many of the other staff members traveled too. They had learned that you can make more impact on a group of citizens by talking to them than by writing letters.

Since there weren't very many of them, they had to spread themselves quite thin, but General Maas and Major McCahill were on tour together occasionally. Bill remembers with a chuckle that he and Mel were once given a three-room hotel suite—two bedrooms with a huge conference room in between. At about three in the morning Bill was awakened by a lot of bumping and thumping in the conference room. He got up and found Maas groping around the walls. "What's the matter, Mel?" he asked.

"I can't find my blanketty-blank bedroom!" the General fumed.

All of Mel's associates love to tell about his self-reliant spirit and his horror about looking or acting "blind." When he appeared at a conference on solving the problems of the handicapped in Louisville, Kentucky, on April 24, 1956, he spoke for himself. After he showed off his cigar-lighting trick for a "Courier-Journal" reporter, he said he was proud of that feat, "but I'm even prouder of my golf. Some of it has improved since I've been blind."

He explained that once he was placed in position, all he needed was a briefing on each hole's terrain. "Blindness cured my hook and slice," he said. "I don't pull my head up when I swing."

He had another surprise. He whipped a collapsible leg of a tripod camera out of his left coat pocket and unfolded it with a flourish. As an admiring audience gathered around, he said, "I use it mainly as a guide. It helps to measure steps when I'm going to go up and down them. And if I stand alone for five minutes or so without touching something, I tend to lose my balance unless I take out my tripod."

During that Louisville conference, Mel Maas spoke at length of the hopes and ideals of the President's Committee on Employment of the Physically Handicapped, emphasizing that he and his colleagues were seeking to find employment for 275,000 handicapped persons each year. "Last year, 200,000 of them were placed," he reported. "I won't be happy, though, until my committee is put out of business;

that is, when people see the value of hiring handicapped people. I don't know if I'll be around to see that day."

He touched on a topic that was close to his heart when he said, "The secret of American business is American ingenuity. And it's the handicapped person who has to rely on his ingenuity."

At one of the luncheon meetings in Louisville, Maas pointed out that every dollar spent on rehabilitation of a handicapped person provides the Government with $10 in tax money when the handicapped person is able to earn a wage. He said it costs $1,500 a year to maintain a handicapped person on public welfare rolls, while only $500 is needed to rehabilitate the same person so he can be employed.

Even though he yearned to be at the controls of a plane again, Major Gen. Maas certainly was not "grounded." As one of the foremost supporters of aviation legislation, he had often stressed the need for high-speed air transportation. As chairman of the President's Committee, that's what he needed most. A 1956 story in "Performance" told about a small portion of the giddy schedule of the blind General, who had already visited most of the states in the Union since taking over the chairmanship in 1954:

On October 2 and 3, 1956, he met with the Oklahoma Governor's Committee in Oklahoma City. The next day he participated in special National Employ the Handicapped Week observances with the New Mexico Governor's Committee at Albuquerque. On

October 5, he was off to Arizona and a date with the Governor's Committee in Phoenix. During the following three days, he made radio and television appearances, met with members of the California Committees, and addressed the International Conference on Employment Security in Los Angeles. His hectic schedule included meetings in Boise, Idaho, on October 9—Helena, Montana, on October 10—and Chicago, Illinois, on October 11. Wherever his plane landed, DAV delegations gathered to welcome General Maas, the immediate past commander of the Disabled American Veterans. DAV members have been active participants in employ-the-handicapped programs.

The Marine Corps Reserve Officers Association continued to be one of General Maas' major interests. He was the star of a traditional ceremony that started back in November 1948, when he first placed MCROA's floral Eagle, Globe and Anchor at the Tomb of the Unknown Soldiers, inaugurating an annual Marine Reserve observance of Nov. 10 as the Marine Corps birthday. The history of "The Marine Corps Reserve, 1916-1966" notes that "It was a solemnly stirring moment in MCROA history, as Colonel Maas marched forward to lay the wreath." Reserves from the various units formed ranks, and the Marine Drum and Bugle Corps played, while Volunteer Marine pilots flew cover overhead.

In 1954, the ceremony was observed at a new location, just outside of Arlington Cemetery. On November 10, the 179th Anniversary of the founding of the Corps, a dramatic new bronze memorial took its place among the historical shrines of Washington. Driving along one of the major highways into the city, travelers feel their hearts beating faster as they glimpse the flag waving triumphantly above the towering cluster of rugged figures.

At close range, the Iwo Jima Memorial is unique in a city crowded with formal white statues. Standing out in breathtaking detail are the heavy Marine boots, the rumpled "utilities" and the grim faces of the five Marines and one Navy corpsman who defied the enemy and the elements to secure the Stars and Stripes atop Mount Suribachi. Sculptor Felix G. W. de Weldon had labored for almost nine years to create that gigantic reproduction of Joe Rosenthal's Pulitzer prize-winning picture.

Because "uncommon valor was a common virtue" in the Corps long before Iwo Jima, the memorial is a tribute to all Marines through history. Regular and reserve Marines from all over the world contributed to the memorial, which was presented to the American people by the Commandant of the Corps. Seven thousand people, including the President and Vice President, witnessed the impressive ceremonies in 1954. Arrangements for the program had been made by two Reserve officers, Lieut. Col. William P. McCahill and Captain Stephen Tripp.

Almost as legendary as the statue itself are some of the stories that surround its creation. While he was working on the statue in his Washington studio, sculptor de Weldon was visited by photographer Rosenthal, who gazed at it with awe and called it "magnificent." The sculptor accepted the compliment with enthusiasm, but added, "Without your picture, Mr. Rosenthal, this would never have been possible."

Rosenthal then reminded him, "Without those Marines, there would have been no picture."

There were some other sprightly utterances in the area of the Iwo Jima memorial on November 10, 1956, when Captain Patricia Maas served as her father's aide during the annual wreath-laying ceremony. Even though General Maas could not see, he realized that Pat had quietly left her olive-green marine overcoat in the car. It was a bitterly cold day, but Pat did not want "to spoil the picture" of all those handsome dress blues assembled for the ceremony. To her, freezing stiff should be "a common virtue" for a lady Marine.

When her father told Pat to get her coat out of the car and put it on, she flatly refused. General Maas turned to Commandant Pate in exasperation and said, "You've got a captain who sasses generals."

"That's nothing," Commandant Pate replied. "She sasses commandants too."

Chapter Sixteen

Years of Progress

The top members of the President's Committee had not always done a great deal of traveling. Early in its history, two meetings a year had been held, drawing attendance from all over the United States. Later, the Committee realized it was not accomplishing enough by bringing people to Washington. It had to go out to the people, so regional meetings were introduced. In addition to the annual spring meeting and the observance of National Employ the Physically Handicapped Week in the fall in Washington, regional meetings started bringing state and local leaders together for discussions of their common problems and achievements. This was a mass innovation and a great one in the various areas of the nation.

It was a successful "personal" approach. Governors' committees agreed unanimously that regional meetings were the most invigorating means of maintaining a high state of activity at the "grassroots" level.

Mel Maas liked the idea of "going out to the people," to encourage them and applaud their triumphs. At Miami's Parade of Progress and Exposition on rehabilitation and employment of the handicapped in 1956, he praised the exposition as an outstanding example of local initiative, saying it was "a symbol of how Florida feels toward the question of providing job opportunity for the physically handicapped. Florida, from its beginnings, has taken upon itself the task of rehabilitating its own broad stretches of shore and swamp until now it has become a modern wonder of the world. Where could you find a better environment for the rehabilitation of the handicapped?"

When job placements for the handicapped were beginning to set respectable records in 1956, General Maas said, "The finest reward of years of effort on the part of thousands of dedicated men and women in the battle to provide job opportunity for the handicapped is the satisfaction of having played a part in this great nationwide program and to know that results are being achieved."

General Maas had tremendous faith in the ability of the clergy to help express his own convictions about rising above handicaps. It was evident that the Rev. Robert J. McCrakken, minister of the Riverside Church in New York City in 1956, had pondered both the spiritual and physical aspects of the subject. Among other significant remarks in one of his sermons, he said:

"We all have handicaps of some sort. They may be physical, mental, temperamental. The important thing is to learn how to handle them. Above everything else, try not to give way to bitterness. The odds against you are doubled if you allow a handicap—poor health, limited opportunity, a personality problem—to make you resentful, your face sullen, your chin down, your shoulders sagging . . . Bitterness is like poison. It is as liable to cause disease as any germ. It breeds touchiness, hypersensitiveness, hostility."

Late in 1956, President Eisenhower appointed General Maas to direct the Committee for the Handicapped of the People-to-People Program for World Understanding. At the first meeting, General Maas told the other members of the committee, "The People-to-People Program is based, in the words of President Eisenhower, 'upon the assumption that no people, as such, want war—that all people want peace.' . . . The President rightly said at our first meeting that this work was very close to the heart of all people, 'except for those few who want unjustly to rule others,' and so, with a watchful eye on the malicious minority who deal in untruth and misunderstanding, we embark upon a glorious mission . . .

"Great masses of people of Asia and Africa are now working to obtain their fair share of the good things of the earth. Communism and democracy are seeking their friendship and support in the cold war and must have it to win . . .

"People working for the rehabilitation of the handicapped are doing as much to forge a great weapon in the cold war as are all the propagandists put together.

"The people of Asia and Africa understand from our deeds, and not from Communist propaganda to the contrary, that we Americans must be decent, generous, kindly people and must have compassion in our hearts . . ."

In and out of the states, and in and out of the country, Mel Maas went forth to blaze new trails in the heartlands of human understanding.

The people on the President's Committee staff cherish the stories that Mel used to bring home from his trips. Once, when he was speaking at the State Capitol in Oklahoma, he knew that the audience included some school children, but he didn't know that they were touring on a tight schedule. After he had talked for about ten minutes, he suddenly heard the tramp-tramp-tramp of marching feet. He had a peculiar feeling all the time he was speaking. "I thought maybe I was talking to an empty room until I finished and heard the applause," he chuckled.

Often he announced at the beginning of a speech, "If any of you want to leave, you can go now—I won't see you."

His approach to an audience was spectacular. "I know how it feels to be handicapped," he would confide. As a sympathetic murmur arose from the audience, he would continue, "Yes, I'm handicapped. I wear false teeth." Sometimes he would even take an oversized set of false teeth from his pocket and park them on the speaker's stand. A wave of laughter would sweep away the first moment of gloom.

As a speaker, Mel Maas knew how to handle humor with dramatic deftness. There was nothing calculating about it—he loved the funny side of life, and he wanted to share it. Sometimes he worried that he might repeat himself to the same audience. "We've got to get some new humor," he would tell his colleagues after a trip. But Mel Maas' jokes never sounded "old." At one point, he added a new twist to his sentiments about women. "A blind man is authorized to kiss every beautiful woman he meets, and all women are beautiful!" he would say.

Because he aroused the affection of his audiences with the leaven of humor, his serious remarks carried more impact. When he welcomed the delegates to the Annual Meeting of the President's Committee in May 1957, General Maas recommended the elimination of members who show little interest, and stepped-up recruiting of active, enthusiastic individuals from management, labor, the professions, the clergy and other groups whose efforts would increase the acceptance of the handicapped as able workers.

"I hope I am not sounding like a professor exhorting his class," he said. "I am telling you these things in the hope that all community committees will begin to think a little more about the many ways and means of implementing our program. We have a fine big diesel engine of a program. All it needs is a lot more fuel and a lot more able engineers at the throttle.

"We are getting more and more spread to our program as more and more community committees become active. I firmly believe that wherever we manage to develop a close working relationship between governors' committees and local committees, we will find significant increases in placements." That spring, the Executive Committee invited the ladies' auxiliaries of the American Legion, VFW, and DAV to membership on the President's Committee.

One of the highlights of the spring meetings was the presentation by the President of the United States of prizes in the National Essay Contest for High School Students. The contests had been a part of the Committee's program since 1949. Among the "working titles" selected by the Committee during those years were: "The Physically Handicapped—Competent, Dependable Workers," "Hiring the Handicapped in Our Town," and "Jobs for the Handicapped, Passports to Dignity."

Although some teachers have been "resistant" to essay contests, Miss Ebbie Whitten's English students at Lake Charles High School in Louisiana won five trips to Washington, a $2,000 scholarship, five sea cruises, a trip to Detroit and several thousand dollars in cash, over a period of ten years. Miss Whitten said, "I have consistently assigned this subject and shall always do so because I feel that the monetary reward in this case is not the most important benefit. The student learns a great and important social lesson and incidentally, also learns much about good writing."

The national essay prizes are contributed by the Disabled American Veterans, and the transportation and expenses for the Washington trip are provided by the AFL-CIO. Mrs. A. B. Cohen of Cincinnati, Ohio, presents the plaques that are given to the five winning high schools.

At the 1957 Annual Meeting, President Eisenhower noted, when he presented the cash prizes, that all five winners of the essay contest were girls. "I hope to see some boys here next year," he said. (There were three young men among the winners in 1958!)

President Eisenhower also complimented General Maas on his inspired leadership of the hire-the-handicapped program during that spring meeting in 1957. Later in the year, on the Committee's tenth anniversary, the President said in a letter of congratulations: ". . . The progress that has been made in rehabilitating and employing the handicapped in the past decade in the close partnership between the dedicated volunteers and equally dedicated professionals has truly made the past ten years the brightest in the history of the handicapped of the United States."

While in Europe attending a Council Meeting of the World's Veterans Federation that year, he also was received at the Vatican by Pope Pius XII who had high praise for the program for hiring the handicapped in the United States. General Maas reported that the Pontiff was in complete agreement with his view that the "language of disability" is a universal language.

When he reached fiscal 1957, General Maas reported on his traveling activities—a fantastic list for a "handicapped" person. In addition to making speeches far and wide, he had completed his three-year plan to visit every state committee in the continental United States. His fellow staff members also had visited with governors, mayors and committee officials; addressed meetings of public and private groups; and provided technical and professional assistance to local and state committees in implementing committee programs.

According to the July issue of "Performance," President Eisenhower, Chairman Melvin Maas, Vice Chairman Earl Bunting, and the weatherman all teamed up to make the 1958 Annual Meeting of the President's Committee a huge success.

General Maas delivered the keynote address at the very moment that headlines in the nation's press told how the General had received final rites from his priest following his collapse in church and hospitalization at Bethesda Naval Hospital the preceding Sunday.

Wasting little time on the state of his own health, Maas spoke buoyantly of "seeing" the next ten years as a golden opportunity for the physically handicapped. He said, "We are going to so seriously need their skills and their abilities that there are very bright days ahead for them."

Pictures of the annual meeting showed General Maas honoring Donald V. Wilson for his years of service as head of the International Society for the

Welfare of Cripples, accepting a box of assorted cheeses sent by the entire student body of Granton, Wisconsin, high school, and presenting the Blinded Veterans Award of the Year to Mr. Sumner Whittier, administrator of Veterans Affairs.

In 1958, there was a breakthrough in one of the greatest areas of concern, job rehabilitation for the epileptic. Epi-Hab, the amazingly successful experiment in providing job opportunities for epileptics, started branching out to other parts of the country from its original Veterans Administration base in Los Angeles. Of special importance is the fact that many of the applicants were veterans who were giving up their life pensions for the sake of a steady job and normal family living. It was noted that the money Epi-Hab had saved the government in relinquished pensions would more than return the money the government had appropriated for Epi-Hab.

In an age when employers still worry that an epileptic employee might fall against a machine during a seizure, Epi-Hab won the Los Angeles Safety Award. It also received a bronze plaque from the Community Chest, because its "fortunate" workers were so generous about contributing to the "unfortunates" of their community. The time lost due to seizures on the job at the plant was an insignificant 100 hours out of 80,000.

General Maas had high praise for a 1958 Government pamphlet, "Help for Handicapped Women," which reported that nearly 90,000 women had been rehabilitated during the preceding four years. "To my knowledge this is the first time that a publication has been prepared specifically to deal with the problems of handicapped women," Maas said. Among special features of the book was a description of the vocational categories open to women who had suffered disabilities. The largest group was employed in the clerical field, and a remarkable number were in professional and technical work.

In July 1958, General Maas was a highly-feted guest in Ketchikan, Juneau, Fairbanks, and Anchorage, Alaska. He had completed "the labor of love" he set for himself three years before, when he resolved to visit every Governor's and Territorial committee. The trip was made by plane, of course, and he spoke to several Seattle groups while he was at it.

Welling Wedemeyer, a student at William L. Dickenson High School in Jersey City, won a poster prize that year. He had pictured a jaunty factory worker marching along to his job with a good-natured grin on his face—and his lunch box swinging from a "hook" that had taken the place of his right hand. The Committee used it nationally.

A star-studded cast of luminaries graced the podium at the Annual President's Committee Meeting in 1959. In his welcoming address, Chairman Maas told the distinguished guests and delegates, "You and I are interested in people as human beings, as individuals. We are concerned not with their production, but with their dignity, and you know no one is doing more in this cause than you are.

"When you help a down-and-out man, dejected because he feels rejected—a handicapped man—the thrill of helping one such person is immense. You can help them by giving them the opportunity to get a job so they can again hold their heads high in the community, and support themselves and their families. You can take them off welfare and put them on the tax rolls—oh, what a thrill, what a reward . . ."

One of the recipients of special recognition from the President's Committee that year was the Cornhusker's Hotel of Lincoln, Nebraska. Among its twenty handicapped employees were men and women with hearing and speech impairments, mental retardation, paralysis of varying severity, epilepsy, and other disabilities—but they were working as successful dishwashing machine operators, bakers and bakers' helpers, maids, cooks, waitresses, timekeepers, kitchen helpers, and housemen.

In 1960, when General Maas was presented with the United States Information Service's Distinguished Service Citation for "outstanding leadership" as Chairman of the People-to-People Committee for the Handicapped, Ambassador George V. Allen noted that "the story of the concern of the American public for rehabilitation and employment of the handicapped is widely known abroad . . ."

When the AFL-CIO announced in 1960 that it would arrange for all the first place state winners in the essay competition to attend the annual meeting, instead of only the top five in the country, Chairman Maas said the "generous act" would be an increased incentive for 11th and 12th grade students to enter the contest. "Future employers and employees and their families are better able to understand the importance of hiring the handicapped as a result of this contest," he declared. "I am sure this continued top-level support by the AFL-CIO will be directly responsible for developing an even more favorable climate of opinion toward the handicapped among all Americans."

One of the most dynamic speakers at the 1960 Annual Meeting was Miss Vivian Acord, Public Information Director of the Indiana Association for Mental Health, who said in part: "I sincerely believe an informed American public, alert to social reality, one day will view mental illness as it does a physical illness. Personally . . . I still think it's a lot of eyewash to say that: 'We no longer regard mental illness as a disgrace.' Sure, we say that, but we don't practice what we preach . . . Consider this tragic example . . .

"As recently as last year just before Mental Health Week, one of the Chicago papers carried a page one story about a nurse at the House of Correction who'd just been fired. It said the nurse had been fired 'reluctantly' after an FBI fingerprint check showed she'd been an 'inmate'—and how I loathe that word—of a mental institution—another word I wish we'd get rid of . . .

"The warden said her record had been excellent, but again I quote: 'In a job like this, we dare not take any chances!' (Whatever he meant by taking chances on a job in a jail, I'll never know.) He added that the nurse was unusually well liked, and that her patients had prompted a letter to the warden, mailed from outside the jail, which asserted: 'A moral wrong has been done to a wonderful woman . . .' "

Among the many business firms championing employment for the handicapped, the Hecht Company lighted up the northern Virginia skyline during July and August 1960, with a huge annual salutation —four stories high and nearly three hundred feet long—reading: "HIRE THE HANDICAPPED! IT'S GOOD FOR THEM AND FOR YOU."

This letter indicated that Warner Brothers studios was helping the cause along: "I thought you might like to know that during the past several months the many thousands of letters directed to our stars, especially the new ones created in our TV series, such as Jim Garner, "Kookie" Byrnes, etc., have swamped our fan mail department. In order to alleviate the situation, we are making it a point to hire the physically handicapped, who are able to work at home. They answer letters, requests for photos, etc. The way it is going right now, it might well develop into another 'industry' for the people in whom you are interested. Probably other companies will follow our example—at least I hope so."

In October 1960, Colonel John Griffin, chairman of the Missouri Committee, established a program to interest all religious faiths and groups in the state's "Hire-the-Handicapped" program. As part of the project, the Catholic, Jewish, and Protestant faiths issued a pamphlet containing statements endorsing a strong employment program for Missouri's handicapped. It included a directory of employment offices.

When General Maas issued his Christmas message that year, it bore some of the earmarks of a "farewell address." He lauded the various activities —NEPH Week, the Annual Committee Meeting, the Seminar, meetings of the Committee on Disabled Veterans, the Public Information, Workmen's Compensation and Mentally Handicapped committees. "Now," he noted almost nostalgically, "we have a new administration moving into Washington. President Kennedy will have my resignation. I have no idea of what action he will take, but whoever takes the helm will inherit a good, basically sound and growing "National Employ the Physically Handicapped" mechanism. I have met with every Governor's Committee the past few years and know you will deliver for any chairman . . ." He concluded by saying, "As before, President Eisenhower thanks you again for your years of selfless service to this great humanitarian cause."

So there was a new young chief executive in the White House. President John F. Kennedy did not accept the resignation that General Maas sent to him.

Considering the state of his health, it is surprising that the blind chairman of the President's Committee did not insist on retiring. He continued to tackle everything with the same enthusiasm and jolly good humor. Once in awhile, he would come into the office and say as he collapsed into a chair, "I'm bushed!"

When staff member Larry Burdick told him he should conserve his energy, a typical answer would be, "I do conserve my energy. I kneel when I take my shower!"

Mel Maas spent part of January and February 1961 in Bethesda Naval Hospital for "a checkup and treatment." The doctors said that cards were okay, but no business. Whether his doctors liked it or not, this was a patient who didn't relax easily.

The General preferred to dress comfortably when he was in his office at home or in the hospital. He probably set some kind of a record for having his picture taken in pajamas and bathrobe—with famous journalists like Bob Considine and other notable individuals.

In February, a bulletin noted that "A hospital bed was the setting and pajamas and bathrobe the uniform of the day as two of the nation's highest civilian honors came to General Maas while he was a patient in the Naval Hospital during January. On each occasion, the audience was as small as the room —one or two of the family, a couple of doctors, one or two members of the President's Committee staff, and the photographers." A citation from President Eisenhower for his major contributions to the cause of the handicapped was conferred by Gerald D. Morgan, former deputy assistant to the President, on January 17. A day later came the Distinguished Service Medal, highest civilian award of the Department of Defense. General Maas each time expressed his appreciation and recognition of the efforts of his fellow volunteers across the country.

The General tried to bounce out of the hospital, with his "tripod cane" unfolded for action, in time for the Annual Spring Meeting. He did fine, except for fainting when he was making his welcoming speech. He curtailed some of his travel activities, but his schedule included the Blinded Veterans Convention in Los Angeles where he wanted to thump the gavel for six days as national president.

It was noted that year that U. S. knowledge concerning the care of the handicapped was being made available to other countries through the People-to-People program: "The hospital ship, Hope, is part of that program. Shipments of artificial limbs to countries in need of such assistance are also part of the program. There is an exchange of information on techniques, treatments and procedures in rehabilitating crippled children and adults." The program had the proud endorsement of Mel Maas, who said, "Nowhere is the humanitarian attitude better demonstrated than in what people do for their unfortunates—their handicapped."

A thorough consciousness of the needs of the handicapped was being developed. According to a report that sounded peculiar at first glance, the United States Department of Agriculture had started designing clothing for handicapped women. It turned out that the "unique collection" was the creation of Clarice Scott, a USDA home economist. The clothing designs, based on extensive research, would help handicapped women to take care of themselves and do their work more efficiently.

The new President in the White House took an

immediate interest in the work of his Committee on Employment of the Physically Handicapped. By September 1961, he had drafted a statement addressed "To Heads of Executive Departments and Agencies." The subject was: "Policy for Employment of the Physically Handicapped." First, he emphasized that "Utilization of physically handicapped persons in productive employment is sound and necessary, both for the contribution handicapped citizens can make to our national productivity, and for the sense of independence and well-being which they can derive from doing a job." Then he reaffirmed "the established employment policy of the Executive branch," and finished with this statement, "The Civil Service Commission will continue to coordinate all phases of this program and will prepare periodic reports of agencies' accomplishments in affording increased employment opportunities to those who are handicapped."

Over the years, promotion of the hire-the-handicapped program had accelerated. The brown and green cogwheel emblem with its slogan, "Ability Counts," had appeared on book matches, shipping cartons, baseball schedules, and on thousands of delivery trucks. Billboards and signs in buses and streetcars were emblazoned with the words, "Jobs for the Handicapped—Passports to Dignity."

When the President's Committee called together some of the nation's leading cartoonists and asked for their assistance in promoting employment of the handicapped through their special talents, General Maas was overwhelmed at the wholehearted response of such famous comic page artists as Milton Caniff of "Steve Canyon" fame, Al Capp of "Li'l Abner," Chic Young of "Blondie," Charles Schulz of "Peanuts," Chester Gould of "Dick Tracy," Mort Walker of "Beetle Bailey," and others, including the cartoonist's committee chairman, Allen Saunders of Mary Worth and Steve Roper fame.

These brilliant, busy people went back to their drawing boards to portray the story of the "hopeful handicapped" with vivid imagery. If there is a moral to this news item, it is the fact that one of the wittiest of the volunteer cartoonists is handicapped himself. Al Capp wears an artificial limb.

Chapter Seventeen

Triumphing Over Stumbling Blocks

The President's Committee has a splendid library of films depicting the progress of its program. Jimmy Jewett, the motion picture technician at committee headquarters, spent several hours showing me tapes of General Maas in action over the years. Here were appealing human interest stories that demonstrated that it is "Ability—not disability—that counts." It would be impossible to give each one the attention it deserves, but no one could skip lightly over the precious minutes when Mel Maas appeared with Helen Keller on Arlene Francis' Home Show.

General Maas went to New York, during the Fortieth Anniversary ceremonies of the American Foundation for Overseas Blind, to present Miss Keller with an award in honor of her lifetime of service to handicapped people. The deaf and blind humanitarian had recently completed a crusade to stimulate interest in the blind in Far Eastern nations.

The award was a plaque, part of which is in braille. Made by students at the Institute for the

Crippled and Disabled in New York City, it cites Miss Keller "for a lifetime of service to humanity and for her example of courage, faith, and triumph over physical obstacles. She has magnificently demonstrated the indestructibility of the human spirit in her successful efforts to advance the employment and social betterment of millions of handicapped people throughout the world."

It was Miss Keller's first appearance on television, and the camera caught a rare moment of radiance that passed much too soon. The beautifully composed face of the lady who had "inspired the handicapped for half a century" was shown on the screen, with an eloquent reading of Milton's sonnet, "On His Blindness," emanating from the background:

When I consider how my light is spent
Ere half my days, in this dark world and wide,
And that one talent which is death to hide
Lodged with me useless, though my soul more bent
To serve therewith my Maker . . .

When Arlene Francis introduced General Maas, she described him as "Not sighted, but he sees so much." The Chairman of the President's Committee spoke that day of the unconscious "prejudice" that confronts the handicapped, although they are the most reliable and loyal people—and the least likely to go drifting from job to job. Helen Keller, he emphasized, was overwhelmingly deserving of the special citation for spreading the messages of peace, understanding, and good will all over the world. She had given new hope to people during her visits to foreign lands. She had demonstrated, by the miracle of her own vibrant presence, that Americans do care about their fellow men.

General Maas' PC colleague and director of the Tufty News Service, Mrs. Esther Van Wagoner Tufty, also appeared on the Home Show program. Out of the conversation came a story she wanted to tell about Helen Keller—"a story so beautiful that if it had happened two thousand years ago it might have been recorded in the Bible. It goes back to that day when she was ten years old, when the light of understanding first crashed through the darkness and the wonderful world opened. She was with her beloved first teacher and constant companion, Ann Sullivan. They were at a water well in the yard of her home in Alabama.

"The teacher took the child's hand and put it beneath the spout of the pump, letting the cool water run over her skin. At the same time she spelled out the word symbol for water on the little girl's hand. Suddenly, for the first time, Helen Keller's mind grabbed at the connection between the symbol and the thing symbolized.

"She dropped to the ground in a fever of excitement and touched it as if to demand the word name for earth. By nightfall of that blessed first day she had the meaning of thirty words.

"What I find most beautiful in this true story is the thought that when God said, 'Let there be light,' and light was denied to Helen Keller, she got something else instead—both Earth and Water on the first day of creation for her."

As Helen Keller had described that miraculous moment, "A little word dropped from my teacher's hand into mine, a ray of light from her soul to set me free."

Also of interest in the projection room was a "hit movie" filmed at the Hughes Aircraft plant at Culver City, California, in cooperation with the President's Committee. "Employees Only" is a close-up study of many handicapped workers employed by Hughes, showing the variety of jobs they are capable of performing.

An important feature of the employees' entrance to the plant is a slanted ramp. A majority of people can skip normally and naturally up and down flights of steps. If they notice a ramp—and most of the government buildings have them now—it is something apart from them. And yet, with millions of crippling accidents every year, the man who trots casually up the stairs to his job today may be grateful for that ramp some other day.

In the opening scene of the Hughes Aircraft film, "Employees Only," which was narrated by Bob Cummings, an attractive young woman was shown driving her car into the parking lot of the huge West Coast plant. She slid deftly toward the right side of the seat, unloaded a collapsible wheel chair and lowered herself efficiently into it—with no assistance at all. Then she wheeled herself toward the ramp at the employees' entrance to the building where she would be performing a full day's work at her desk. A former polio patient, she would not be sitting at a lonely window watching the rest of the world go about its business.

Hughes Aircraft has been a pioneer in the employing of the handicapped because it "pays." Howard Hughes began to hire the handicapped as a humanitarian gesture. Now his company has a staff of special interviewers to search out the skills and potentialities of disabled job applicants. It is no longer a matter of being kind to the "less fortunate." It is good business on the profit side of the ledger. These people are skilled and diligent. As General Maas so often pointed out, a person is only handicapped if he loses his dignity and self-respect—if he is unable to use his ingenuity and talents.

In the Hughes plant, all the disabled employees had earned the right to the jobs they held. There was a paraplegic who was a skilled welder, and a computer operator who slept in a respirator at night. One engineer, a former big league pitcher who had lost a leg when he was shot down over Germany during World War II, sometimes played ball with the company team. Another former athlete pioneered a wheel chair basketball team.

Among the employees was a man with cerebral palsy who was once considered completely unemployable. The blind perform delicate jobs with their hands. Those without hands have been fitted with prosthetic devices that make them "handy" at precision work.

Mel Maas emphasized, in his remarks as commentator on the Hughes film, that it's not what a man doesn't have, but what he does with what he has left that counts. This may even have applied to an occasional "wheel chair romance" in the Hughes plant, with a happy domestic life to follow.

Speaking for themselves, the handicapped workers said that they are not "pampered" and they do not expect special privileges and treatment. They wanted to be accepted as workers, not as objects of "do-goodism."

Maas also noted that disabled persons concentrate their other healthy faculties on the job before them. It is a case of "compensation plus." That was one reason why the Hughes workers kept piling up production records leading to many promotions.

The Hughes film proved to be a "spectacular." After its premiere showing in Washington, TV stations began clamoring for prints. The Navy Department asked Hughes for an OK to make between fifty and seventy-five additional prints for training and orientation use and for promoting more jobs for the handicapped in Navy installations around the world.

At every opportunity, the Chairman of the President's Committee stressed the safety records of physically impaired persons. Insurance companies agreed that they are good risks, and Mel Maas had the figures to prove it. The disabled are more likely to keep alert, and they are careful because they have already learned to beware of accidents that might lead to further disability. They work harder and set high performance standards for themselves. They are not only proving their worth to their employers; they are also proving their worth to themselves as they build up self-confidence in the face of each new day's challenge.

During a filmed visit with executives of Employers' Mutuals of Wausau in Madison, Wisconsin, General Maas was asked about his handicap. "I'll never be handicapped as long as I have my voice," he quipped. He had gone to Madison to present the President's Committee's top honor, the Distinguished Service Award, to an insurance firm that had pioneered in hiring the handicapped back in 1928 and had continued to promote the expansion of "education" among both employers and handicapped throughout the state.

J. M. Sweitzer, president of Employers' Mutuals, explained the philosophy of his company this way: "The real argument against class discrimination in employment policy, whether its victims be handicapped workers or any other 'labeled' group . . . is purely economic. It is not social or moral or legal . . . No businessman can afford the luxury of discrimination."

As Chairman of the President's Committee, Mel Maas was deeply conscious of the multiple handicaps that the handicapped must face—above and beyond their own handicaps. His emotions were best expressed by a prize-winning poster that was prominently displayed during those years. It showed a young man in a wheel chair looking upward in dismay at the high, steep flight of stairs before him. Because of those stairs, the door at the top would always be closed to him.

"One of the most frustrating problems confronting disabled persons is to be denied access to public buildings and facilities whose design prohibits full participation by the physically handicapped," according to a review of the situation in "Performance." "This problem is equally frustrating to rehabilitation personnel. The finest programs of rehabilitation, education or recreation are unavailable to the disabled if they cannot have access to the very buildings they need to enter to use these services."

General Maas recalled that the President's Committee's interest in the problem and concern for its solution actually started when the late Hugo Deffner of Oklahoma City was brought to Washington in 1957 to be honored as the "Handicapped American of the Year." The monumental architecture of the auditorium where he was to meet the President, however impressive, was an unmanageable "obstacle course" for Deffner's wheel chair until some husky Marines carried him up the steps.

The walls wouldn't need to come tumbling down, but architectural barriers would need to be smoothed out. The Advisory Council, which met at the White House under Chairman Maas, became involved in studying the problem. The Employment Service, the Veterans Administration and other alert groups analyzed the situation and gave it widespread publicity. Someone observed, "Stores are built with street-level entrances. Why not public and other business places?"

Enlightened "barrier publicity" included this charming little verse which appeared in "Architectural Blocks in School Buildings," published by the Illinois Commission for Handicapped Children:

> To each is given a kit of tools,
> A shapeless mass and a book of rules,
> And each will build ere the final call,
> A stumbling block or a door for all.

Although there is still so much to be done in so many areas, there is cause for rejoicing at the imaginative cooperation that has been received from some major business and government leaders.

In 1960, General Maas was able to report to President Eisenhower that progress toward equipping all public buildings with ramps and handrails for the convenience of the handicapped was being made. He would have been even more optimistic if he could have peered ahead into the future at that time. The following few examples indicate that the barrier problem has been tackled with zeal in a variety of unrelated architectural areas and localities:

Of special interest in February 1962, was the news that New York's handsome new Lincoln Center for the Performing Arts would have all entrances at street level; every floor accessible from large attendant-operated elevators; special parking near exits reserved for the handicapped; seats that can be removed to accommodate wheel chairs, and transistor amplifiers for those requiring hearing aids.

The Canadian Labor Department reported in 1963 that the Canadian Paraplegic Association and other Canadian groups are engaged in efforts to remove architectural barriers to the handicapped. Examples included the new O'Keefe Centre for Performing Arts in Toronto, Fort Garry Church and Public Library, and a bowling alley in Halifax—all built with the handicapped in mind.

In February 1964, the Governor of Minnesota signed into law a bill which specified that all new state government buildings must be constructed with consideration for the handicapped—ramps instead of stairs, wide doors, and other facilities that will make buildings more accessible and usable for everyone. At that time, Minnesota was the fourteenth state to take action through legislation or resolution.

In May 1964, it was learned that there would be "doors for all" in Equitable Life's magnificent new $25 million building in Chicago. "The new 35-story skyscraper will be Chicago's first new building planned specifically to accommodate the handicapped. Certain parking spaces will be marked solely for the handicapped. Doorknob grooves will warn the blind of dangers ahead. Drinking fountains and phones will be at wheel chair level; doors will be wide enough for wheel chairs and will have horizontal handrailings. A landscaped plaza will provide ground-level entrances to the building so that handicapped, aged, and patients with heart conditions can alight from a car, enter the building, and walk or roll straight to an elevator."

In December 1965, word was received that the Trustees of the National Gallery of Art in Washington, had agreed to the installation of a ramp for the assistance of handicapped visitors.

Millions of visitors have made a pilgrimage to a gravesite in Arlington Cemetery since late in November 1963. In 1966, it was announced that there will be a specially designed walkway for handicapped persons to enable them to reach the permanent monument more easily after its completion. All this, in 1960, was "history in the future."

Larry Burdick, the editor of "Performance," believes that Mrs. Evelyn Taylor may have been "responsible" for the ramp and automatic doors at the eastern end of the huge Department of Labor Building. She was in publications work in Michigan and was employed for a time in the U. S. Printing Office. Now editorial assistant in the offices of the President's Committee, Mrs. Taylor types at her desk and gets around in her small collapsible wheel chair more efficiently and unobtrusively than most people who walk, and she has a talent for anticipating exactly the type of memo or publication that is required at the moment. In other words, she makes her bosses look good. She has been employed on the President's Committee staff for just about as long as the wheel chair ramp has been in operation, and she has piled up an amazing record of steady job attendance.

Mr. Burdick says the President's Committee has had to deal with a variety of problems—including romantic disasters. There was the time a Catholic nun called from a northern state to report the ill-starred elopement of two very young people who were far from home. There had been an automobile accident, and the twenty-year-old bridegroom was in the hospital completely paralyzed. His fifteen-year-old bride was frightened and miserable.

After the President's Committee had arranged for the youngsters to be returned to their home city in the South, a "publicity campaign" was launched through the cooperation of their local radio station. Soon the young man had a job taking orders for a local rug cleaning firm from a prone position in bed. The telephone company installed an automatic diaphragm on his chest, because he was unable to work with anything but his voice. Oh, yes, the Committee even became involved in reconciling the parents of the young people to an acceptance of the marriage.

Summing it up in the words of General Maas, "Creating an employment climate for handicapped people requires the cooperation of professionals and volunteers in every community in the country."

Rehabilitation Administration figures show there are about two million physically disabled men and women who require vocational rehabilitation but are not getting it for the following three reasons: "Many of the disabled do not know that such services are available, individual states do not provide the 'matching money' to implement the federal program, and the necessary medical and vocational facilities are not available." And it adds, "But all of these reasons can be grouped under one big reason—lack of public support."

Viewed from any direction, the problems of employment of the handicapped are never a cut-and-dried matter because there is too much human nature involved. This author noted that Mel Maas, on several occasions, became impatient at the thought of blind and crippled people sitting on sidewalks soliciting charity. "What about that?" I asked Bernie Posner. "Was he disturbed about lack of facilities for training them to do something more dignified?"

"Almost any handicapped person in the country can get training—if he really insists on it," Bernie said.

"You mean that some of them don't want it?"

There followed an enlightening explanation of the reason why some handicapped persons "give up." They know of others who have gone to training centers and applied themselves industriously to developing a skill. Sometimes it was a long, frustrating ordeal, but they rejoiced at each small triumph as they looked forward with hope and enthusiasm to the day when they would have jobs again. But too often that day has never come. There has been too much employer resistance to hiring the handicapped—to giving them the chance that they have tried so hard to earn. Why not just sell pencils or hold a tin cup, and be done with it? As though it is not enough to lose one's legs or one's eyesight, there is the added heartbreak of "not being wanted."

In his speeches, General Maas emphasized over and over again that employers need "educating" as much as the disabled do. He recognized that the employment market was not always stable and that sometimes there were too many applicants for each job, but he believed that every effort should be made to give rehabilitated persons an equal chance to demonstrate their skills and abilities. In a great variety of jobs, a man does not need the physique of a "Mr. America," and a disabled person may be more highly qualified for some positions than a dozen Adonises.

"It would be a cruel hoax on the individual and a fraud upon the taxpayer to spend public funds for vocational rehabilitation if there is no job opportunity for those rehabilitated men and women," Mel Maas insisted.

Many distinguished American business firms—large and small—have come to realize that "It Pays to Hire the Handicapped." There are thousands of them on the payroll at Du Pont, Ford, Caterpillar Tractor, Bendix, Ace Electronics and Sears, Roebuck—to name only a few—and their employers agree that they "pull their own weight" on the job.

As for the handicapped employees, they get a feeling of achievement from those three little words: "On the payroll!"

Chapter Eighteen

Fond Recollections

A recent visit with some members of the PC staff produced a deluge of anecdotes about General Maas' invincible spirit — and his supercharged sense of humor.

Among the "spontaneous" participants was Colonel Bill McCahill, executive secretary of the President's Committee, who had been close to him for so many years in the Marine Corps Reserve Officers Association and had known that Mel Maas would fill the office of Chairman of the President's Committee to perfection. He had seen the way the older man had made his peace with his blindness—a fantastic adjustment when almost everything he loved to do, including flying a plane, depended on his eyesight.

There was Harold Russell, whose name has been familiar to movie-goers ever since "The Best Years of Our Lives," which is now being shown to television night owls. No one who has seen that picture will ever forget Harold's Oscar-winning portrayal of the young man who came home from World War II with mechanical metal appliances instead of hands, and who was in a state of anguish because he did not know whether there was love—or pity—waiting for him. The role was poignantly appropriate; Sergeant Harold Russell had lost his hands during a wartime training accident.

Harold looks just about the same as he did when he was everybody's "favorite movie actor." I had been wondering about the proper way to greet a man who had no hand to shake, but Harold arose from behind his desk with a big grin, swung his arm toward me with a flourish, and I "shook the hook" and was promptly charmed by his magnetic personality.

Harold Russell had met General Maas in 1950 and had immediately been impressed by his talents as a leader—as a "take charge guy"—who was quick to analyze problems and reach constructive conclusions. Mel's memory for facts, figures, and funny stories was fabulous, especially after he became blind. As he often said, "That's because I'm not handicapped by eyesight." Harold recalled that his comprehension of time was remarkable. When he was asked to talk for sixty seconds on TV, he finished in exactly fifty-nine.

There were no dull moments when Mel was around. Harold will never forget the time he and the blind General were in Berlin together. They were being driven through the city by a taxi driver who kept squinting ahead in the traffic and weaving a zigzag course. At last the driver mentioned that he was having trouble with his eyes and could hardly see. This struck Mel Maas as uproariously funny, because he could picture himself at the wheel in that hectic Berlin traffic.

When he and Harold would be leaving a hotel room, Mel would say, "Don't bother to turn out the lights"—just as though he could see whether they were off or on.

There was an unconscious gallantry in his laughing approach to his own disabilities—and to those of other people. After Harold Russell was in the office quite frequently as vice chairman of the President's Committee, he would sometimes greet the General with a playful tweak on the neck, and Mel would whoop, "Hey, those hooks are cold this morning!" or "Here's Russell—I'm getting hooked again!" Once when he was being photographed with Harold and another amputee, he said, "Now I'm being hooked from both sides."

Mel's story of the "Guatemalan incident" is a top favorite with the members of the President's Committee. That was the time when the famous "solo traveler" really got tripped up.

There were supposed to be some government officials, as well as a bevy of attractive young ladies, waiting to meet him when his plane landed in the capital city of Guatemala in the country of the same name. Absolutely no one was there, so Mel followed the other passengers into the terminal by the sound of their footsteps. Still no one came up to welcome him.

There he was in a strange airport terminal that

he could not see, with his ears ringing with a foreign language he could not understand. It was exasperating, but he did not go into a panic. Fortunately he remembered the name of the hotel where he had a reservation, so he began calling out, "San Carlos Hotel!" That would have been fine, except that people must have thought he was a "barker" for the hotel and they ignored him.

After about a half hour, when he was really beginning to feel helpless, an intuitive taxi driver finally figured out his problem and took him to the San Carlos Hotel. His hosts were devastated when he called them—they had not expected him until the next day. After a barrage of apologies, they asked what they could do to make amends. "Send me up a bottle of good Scotch," said the still-shaken General, who later laughed heartily whenever he described the ordeal.

Maas was due to address an Inter-American conference during that trip. In preparing for formal speeches, he usually transcribed his notes in braille and memorized them. He had used the same system when he testified before Congress during his early blind years, and he would chuckle as he "felt" the looks of consternation on the faces of reporters who asked for copies of his text.

While most people seem content merely to exist, Mel Maas wanted to live—vibrantly. He would not even tolerate dull pictures in his "inner mind." Bernie Posner recalled that the longer the General was blind, the more he lost his memory for the way things actually looked—but he kept getting visions of the world around him "in technicolor," as he put it.

The first thing he asked when he entered a room was, "Where's the ash tray?" Everyone recalled his star performance on the Georgetown Forum TV program when—in addition to making some pointed remarks about the skills and talents of the handicapped—he aimed unerringly at the ash tray and turned his face attentively toward each of the other speakers. He had so much skill and talent that viewers couldn't believe he was blind.

Obviously there was some speculation, during those years, about the possible permanency of Mel's blindness. After one gruelling flood of dictation, Dottie Dunnigan said she pointed her finger at her forehead and clicked her tongue as though she were ready to blow her brains out. One of the office gang asked afterward, "What if the General had regained his eyesight right then?"

Mel loved to tell about the time he came home unexpectedly when Mrs. Maas and another lady were "trying on dresses or something." When she saw him in the doorway, the visitor started making embarrassed noises. "Don't worry, I can't see anything," Mel assured her. "But if I could, I wouldn't let you know!"

His colleagues had heard about a classic episode at Hines, when the General was being rehabilitated. One of the Red Cross girls persuaded him to be her partner during a compulsory dancing session for blind patients. While they were dancing, the young lady asked how he was getting along at Hines, and he confided that he was having some difficulty with braille. "Well, be sure you confine your practice to paper," she told him.

The funniest part, according to Mel, was the way his wife asked him, "What did she mean?"

Much has been said and written about the Maas technique of "brailling" his hotel room as soon as he got inside. When he so often traveled alone, he would ask the bellhop to take him on a complete tour of the room to help him locate the telephone, temperature controls, closet, and various pieces of furniture. "Brailling the bathroom" consisted of zeroing-in on everything from the tub or shower faucets to the outlet for his electric razor.

The General always asked for a small room. Because of his VIP status, bighearted hotel managers often arranged to give him the largest suite in the place. With a VIEW!

Once he was traveling with a PC colleague who asked for an eight-dollar room and got it. The General was deposited in more lavish quarters. Mel contrived a swap, and he thought it was funny when his companion, Vince Hippolitus, got stuck with a bill for twenty-five dollars.

All the people at that informal meeting had witnessed the increasing burden of afflictions that Mel Maas carried with such exuberant nonchalance. They recounted them with awe. In spite of having lost three fourths of his ulcer-aggravated stomach on the operating table, he ate and drank with gusto. His false teeth often made his mouth sore. Sometimes he would put a napkin to his face to slide them into his mouth before he made a speech.

He was on a sugar-free diet because he had diabetes, and on a salt-free diet because of his serious heart condition. He had suffered six acute heart attacks. He couldn't use a braille typewriter because his fingers were becoming so stiffened from arthritis. On top of all that, he was blind. When one of the doctors at Johns Hopkins was asked about the General's health, he threw up his hands and exclaimed, "He's a museum of pathology!"

There were times when people wondered at the spirit that kept so remarkable a body in motion. On a number of occasions, he was given the last rites of the church. When he collapsed at the Annual Meeting in 1961, everyone expected him to be in the hospital for months. They were startled to see him at his desk a few days later.

Before he went on trips, Mrs. Maas would assemble packets of pills and medicine, all carefully marked with braille labels. There were eyedrops for the eye irritation that was getting worse, as well as a spectacular assortment of pills for his wide variety of ailments. Once in awhile Mel would casually toss ten or twelve pills into his mouth at once to save keeping track of them. After his hands became so crippled with arthritis, that trick didn't work so well —he would miss his mouth and some of the pills would go rolling merrily away on the floor of the plane.

Still he kept going, full of bubbling life and indestructible humor—more alive at the age of sixty-four than most healthy men half his age. He would come into the office wearing something new. "That's a beautiful red vest," someone would say.

"The h-ll it is," he would retort, "it's blue!"

Mrs. Maas had sewed braille labels in all his clothing, and he rarely got mixed up on his color combinations.

Harold Russell was not putting on a "demonstration" when he was picking up papers and lighting his own cigarettes during that visit, because he does it all the time. It is even more amazing to see him handling silverware and a water glass with such casual dexterity. With typical President's Committee hospitality, I was taken along to a farewell luncheon for Mrs. Sylvia Howard, who was retiring as director of women's activities for the President's Committee.

During subsequent visits, there was more "Maas lore" available. Larry Burdick recalled that the General didn't care much about being called "Maas"—perhaps because it often came out "moss." There wasn't any moss growing on him. He preferred to have his thousands of friends call him "Mel" or "General."

Rosemary Hunt, one of the secretaries, remembers engaging in some whimsical dialogues with the General, often via the dictaphone machine. She sometimes served as his "eyes" in describing pictures that might be used in Committee publications. There was one hilarious period when they were trying to identify a "mystery man" from the only portion of his anatomy that showed up in a group picture—a piece of his ear. The General kept asking Rosemary if she had found any clues to "the rest of that fellow."

Naturally General Maas was curious about the way new acquaintances looked, after he had met them and heard their voices. From the glint of mischief in Rosemary's eyes, she must have come up with some descriptions that were humdingers. It's a point worth pondering—how do people "look" to someone who hears only their voices?

In a delightful article entitled "How NOT to Help the Blind," which was published in "The American Legion Magazine," General Maas gave some pointed advice on the fine art of reading to blind people: "If you are reading to us in public, do it as unobtrusively as you can. We don't appreciate your reading in such a way as to make clear to every passer-by that you're doing a good deed for some 'helpless blind guy.'

". . . Among the best readers of comics I have ever met was an eleven-year-old girl who sat next to me on a plane from Chicago to Washington. After we became acquainted, she began reading her comic books to me. Thoughtfully, she gave me a brief but adequate description of each picture, and she read with remarkable feeling and interpretation. I enjoyed it immensely, and was sorry when the flight came to an end."

"How NOT to Help the Blind" is filled with all the pathos and comedy that was as natural to Mel

Maas as breathing. The complete text of the highly informative article, condensed here, was reprinted by the President's Committee as a public service. The General got down to business in the first paragraph: "The one thing the blind wish people with sight would remember is this: The blind cannot see."

He asked readers to remember the Golden Rule. "If you were blind, how would you want to be helped? . . . Let's say you are going to escort a blind person. Please, don't grab him by the forearm and shove him ahead of you. This may give you the strong, good feeling of helping, but you're being anything but helpful.

"When you 'escort' us that way, we are out in front of you, and, therefore, we never know what's coming—curbstones, slopes, doorways, steps, trees, fire hydrants, telephone poles, people, dogs, cats, what-have-you.

"The proper way is to have the blind person take your arm and follow slightly behind you.

"In this way, we will pretty well know everything you're going to do—start, stop, turn right, turn left, go upstairs, go downstairs, pause to eye a pretty blonde. An almost imperceptible movement of your arm telegraphs to us what's to come. You didn't know that, did you?"

At first General Maas tried to teach people the proper way to escort a blind person, but he was often in the company of three or four different strangers a day and it was impossible to "educate" them all. "I recall returning from trips of two to three weeks—in a different city every day, being 'led' by as many as forty different people—with everything from bruised shins to broken ribs," he noted wryly.

What about stairs? "Some sighted people count out loud—and so very, very loud—the number of steps, one by one. The counting is wasted. All it accomplishes is our complete mortification . . . When we approach a flight of stairs or a curb, it's helpful if you 'square around' so that you and we are both facing the steps or curb head on . . . It might surprise you to realize how easy it is to fall when we think we're at right angles with a step and we're not . . .

"We blind often debate in private whether it's better to fall down or fall up. Personally, I prefer to fall down. It at least gives me the chance to regain my balance before I actually hit ground. I've been remarkably lucky in recovering balance in downward falls . . . and have had some lulus falling up flights of stairs. To tell the truth, the blind don't fall very gracefully up or down. So square us off in order that we don't have to make the choice."

Doorways are a hazard. "If you are guiding the blind person the right way, he is alongside of you, a step or so behind. When you come to a door, he needs as much space to enter as you. Sometimes, without thinking, you walk in blithely, while he bumps suddenly into the door jamb. The proper thing to do is turn and step sideways, particularly if the doorway is rather narrow. The blind person will do likewise, even without being told. The upshot: no bruised bodies."

He was just as eloquent on the subject of hearing: "Many people shout at us, rather than speak to us in a normal tone. We can't see, and somehow they think we can't hear either . . .

"Other people won't speak directly to us. They address themselves to our companions. The stewardess on a plane, for example, might ask the fellow next to me: 'What's his name? How far is he going?' Or a waiter will ask my sighted friend: 'What does he want to eat?'

"You can speak to us; we won't bite you.

". . . We are trained to look directly at the source of a voice, but occasionally we do get crossed up. I recall many a time conducting an animated conversation with the amplifier of a loudspeaker, looking it squarely in the eye, thinking it was a person, while the person himself was away off in some other corner of the hall, talking into a microphone . . ."

At parties, Mel Maas warned, "Don't ever put a glassful of liquid—spirituous or otherwise—in front of me without telling me. If I don't know it's there, I'm apt to knock it over. Also, don't refill my coffee cup with scalding coffee without informing me. I'm likely to take a big gulp, thinking it's as cool as when I last sipped it . . .

"If the dinner includes steak or roast beef or some such, don't hesitate to offer to cut it up for us. Believe me, we won't be embarrassed, after all, we blind like to eat, too . . . And please, if you cut our meat, place the fork in our other hand. That way we won't have to grope for it and possibly come up with a handful of gravy instead . . ."

On the subject of hotel rooms, he told about a "hair-raising experience"—and it wasn't in Guatemala. "I was accompanied to my hotel room by a group that had met me at the airport," he said. "Thoughtfully, someone took my hat and coat, hung them up in the closet and steered me over to a chair. Only whoever it was forgot to tell me where the closet was. We had a lively discussion of what I was to talk about at a luncheon the next day, and I was never given the chance to familiarize myself with the room.

"After all had gone, I prepared for bed. Before taking off my suit, I opened what I thought was the closet door. 'My,' I thought, 'what a large walk-in closet.' As soon as I stepped in, the door snapped shut behind me. I couldn't open it. Imagine my consternation when I discovered that I was out in the hall . . .

"It was midnight, and not a soul was around. I felt my way up and down the hall, listening at doors in the hope that I would hear somebody not asleep whom I could ask for help. Not a sound.

"I began to worry that somebody might see me and call the police to report a sneak thief, a prowler or a Peeping Tom. By this time I had lost track of my own room. I looked for the elevators, but either I was too far from them to hear them, or they had stopped running for the night.

"Then came one of those rare instances of good luck. I bumped into a table on which there was a house phone. I called the desk and explained my plight. Soon, a bellboy arrived with another key. I greeted him like a long-lost brother.

"Now I put the key in my pocket as soon as I check in; and I insist on a room near the elevator. This also enables me to navigate to the lobby by myself . . ."

Mel Maas was a man with a very sick body and a sublimely healthy mind when he wrote that article. At the age of sixty-four, he could say, "For ten years I have been totally blind, and I have developed more of an insight into people in that short decade than in my previous fifty-four years."

Chapter Nineteen

Panorama of Achievement

The first feature of the Annual Meeting in 1962 was a musical program by the United States Marine Band, the organization in which John Philip Sousa took so much pride. The meeting was opened by Mrs. Esther Van Wagoner Tufty. After the Joint Armed Forces Color Guard presented the colors, William Jones of the Marine Band sang the Star-Spangled Banner.

Many members of the PC Executive Committee—an impressive list of leaders in industry, public service and education—were present. After the invocation, Mrs. Tufty introduced a host of distinguished guests on the platform, and Kenneth Pohlman of the United Mine Workers of America Welfare and Retirement Fund delivered the Roll Call of States.

Then Mrs. Tufty announced, "We all love the next speaker. We all respect him. We all look to him when our enthusiasm needs recharging. He sees more than most people who can see. Ladies and gentlemen, the Chairman of the President's Committee, Major Gen. Melvin Maas."

He could not see his audience, but he was inspired by the expectant hush to make a joke of his collapse the year before. "Thank you, Mrs. Tufty, distinguished guests, and fellow taxpayers. As I was saying when I was so rudely interrupted last year—I might say interrupted by myself . . . For some of you who may not have been here last year, in the middle of my welcoming address people thought I fainted. Well, I will tell you what really happened. I have made this same talk so many times that when I heard myself making it again, I got so bored I just fell asleep." This witticism was greeted with laughter and applause.

"What I was saying last year," he continued, "was that in the nearly fifteen years of this committee, of Governors' Committees, and of a considerable number of Mayors' Committees, these committees have come to be recognized as established institutions in this country, as much a part of our structure as any veterans' organization or chamber of commerce, or any other group.

"Our crusade, thanks to you, has become so successful that hiring the handicapped has become part of the way of life of America. It is much more than merely because we are helping the individual to get a job. It is WHY we do it; WHY it is so important for the individual to get a job. Everyone has a deep need to 'belong.' The handicapped person who is rejected by society, or who thinks he's rejected, just doesn't feel that he belongs. Once he can get a job, then that feeling of belonging comes to him. Then his value as a human being, his worth, becomes recognized. That is the heart and essence of American democracy."

At that moment, he touched on a significant new development. ". . . This past year has been one of growth. The President recently broadened our mission . . . We are now the President's Committee on Employment of the Handicapped. The word 'Physically' has been dropped. We have organized a special section to deal with the problems of acceptance of the mentally retarded and the mentally restored.

"We have had a great measure of success in getting employers to accept the physically handicapped, and we hope to have the same measure of success with the mentally restored and mentally retarded.

". . . During the year, we accomplished the major objective in getting building standards adopted by the American Standards Association . . . We started with the Government, and from now on every new Government building will have to conform to the standards. There will be street level entrances, elevators that can be operated by a person in a wheel chair, toilets so arranged that people with ambulatory handicaps can use them, and many other things.

"The Government also has agreed to try to alter existing Government buildings, at least to get a street level entrance, or a ramp, that can be used by those in wheel chairs.

"But we are going far beyond that. We want to get these standards adopted by every state and every municipality, so that all buildings which the public uses will ultimately be available to the handicapped.

"During this year, we launched a new campaign of enlisting the support of women's organizations . . . Its purpose is to see that every person in the country understands the problems of the handicapped and the necessity for creating broader job opportunities for them."

There was also a new program dealing with agricultural workers, General Maas explained. "They comprise no more than 10 per cent of our population; yet they have far more than their share of crippling accidents. Little is known about the problems of rehabilitation and job placement of those on farms. Should handicapped farm workers be re-educated for some other job they can do on the farm? Should they be rehabilitated and vocationally trained so they can work in the city? These are some of the questions we shall study.

"All these are great movements forward . . . If we can just have the same progress in the future as we have been having in the past, we know we shall do this job that is expected of us; the job that the President has charged us with doing; that the Congress has given us the money to do."

There were speeches, panel discussions and workshops dealing with all the complex human problems that are the concern of the President's Committee and its nationwide "partners" during that Annual Meeting.

The keynote speaker was Dr. Leonard W. Mayo,

chairman of the President's Panel on Mental Retardation, who emphasized the importance of omitting the word "Physically" from the title of the President's Committee. "I am keenly concerned," he declared, "with the problems that exist for some of the five million people in the United States who have a degree of mental retardation. We must be conscious of the needs of these people—far more conscious than we have been.

"I may say to you, and I think you know it: many people with a certain degree of mental retardation are now employed in competitive and gainful employment . . .

"This means, my friends, that we are coming to a point in the United States of America where we will one day have the same concern for ALL people and their special needs as we now have for SOME people who stand out because of their special needs . . .

"I suppose to live in an era of great issues, and to have no part in their solution, is really tantamount to not having lived at all. We have a lot of great issues—the exploration of outer space, our relations to other nations of the world, serious domestic problems.

"But I think in the final analysis, my friends, it comes down to the most basic issue of all—a haunting question which has to do with people—whether we accept them or whether we reject them, particularly when they are different than we are in any respect . . ."

Another outstanding speaker, David Brinkley of NBC, lauded Emik A. Avakian, "Handicapped American of the Year"—who had started out as a little Armenian boy who had no use of his arms, hands, or fingers, but who became the inventor of the automatic railroad bridge that could be operated with an electric eye. "A crippled boy with a vastly superior brain," he went through high school and college and received his master's degree from Columbia University. "Somewhere along the way, he decided that communication in his painful, halting speech was too slow and inaccurate. So what did he do? He invented a typewriter that he could operate with his breath!" That, Mr. Brinkley noted, was just one example of meeting the physical obstacle and using your intellectual powers to overcome it.

It was a significant springtime for a number of reasons. Early in 1962, the Labor Department's Regional Directors met in Washington for talks on several forthcoming programs, including the $435,000,000 Manpower Development and Training Act for moving long-termed unemployed into jobs. Far from denouncing legislation of that type as a threat to taxpayers' pocketbooks, General Maas saw it as an opportunity for more Americans to become wage-earning taxpayers. He called the Act "A powerful new tool to alleviate long-term unemployment," and added, "Governors' and Mayors' Committees must remain alert that these opportunities shall be available to the handicapped on the same basis as the able-bodied."

Most of the speakers at the Annual Meeting had noted the special significance of Valentine's Day that spring. Meeting with General Maas at the White House to honor the National Association of Broadcasters for its splendid support of the handicapped program, President Kennedy had chosen "the day of the heart" to remove the word "Physically" from the name of the President's Committee—"because we do want to emphasize the great importance of hiring people who may have suffered some degree of difficulty mentally."

On TV, radio and in the press, the word went out to America and the world that the least of these our brethren—the most socially ostracized and forlorn—were officially welcomed into the human family. It was not a new philosophy within the President's Committee, where all the disabled are seen as "whole" people. It would mean continued broadening of the "grass-roots" base all over the country, but that is the hopeful policy that keeps the President's Committee functioning. It cheerfully chips away at the strongholds of prejudice and does not grow weary of trying to move mountains of public opinion.

A recent PC brochure points out that strong Governors' Committees and strong local committees are the keys to promoting job opportunities for the handicapped. There are a thousand local committees composed of representatives of management, labor, veterans, women's organizations, mass media, educators, the clergy, private and public employment and rehabilitation agencies, mental health, mental retardation, and insurance groups. According to the brochure, "Vigorous local committees can bring new hope to the handicapped. With a stirring mission like that, no wonder there are a thousand local committees in our land." But it was noted, "A thousand more are needed."

The brochure listed the exciting "sampler of activities" that keeps the President's Committee bustling with high-spirited energy all the year around. There is a continuous public service program which is made possible through the cooperation of the Advertising Council, the National Association of Broadcasters, the Veterans Administration and related agencies. Local TV and radio stations, and local newspapers, are ready and willing to carry the story of the handicapped into every home. But the guiding impetus must originate somewhere, and it must have the active support of a vast network of dedicated persons.

Dedicated persons? In every city and town there are lonely women who complain about "unfriendliness," and they usually mean they haven't been invited to join a bridge club. There is no unfriendliness or loneliness for people who step forward and say, "What can I do to help the handicapped in my area?"

In its "activities portfolio," the President's Committee has a handsome assortment of exhibits for specific audiences — posters, billboards, car cards, and magazine literature.

In addition to the annual essay contest prizes, there is this list of spectacular President's Committee Awards, for which nominations must be recommended by Governors' Committees:

The President's Trophy (to the handicapped American who has overcome his handicap and has helped to inspire the employment of other handicapped persons); Employer of the Year Awards (to the large and small firm making the most outstanding records of hiring the handicapped); Public Personnel Award (to the person employed by a public agency or public school system doing the most to encourage employment of the handicapped); Physician's Award (to the physician who has made the most exceptional contributions toward job equality for the handicapped); Distinguished Service Award (for any organization, agency, or individual performing outstanding work in advancing employment of the handicapped); Citation for Meritorious Service (to the organization or individual making an exceptional contribution to the objectives of the President's Committee); and the Employer's Merit Award (in recognition of an exceptional record for hiring the handicapped).

In addition to all that, states may establish their own awards programs. The state and local Sertoma and La Sertoma clubs of Colorado sponsor an annual "Miss Handicapped of America" contest, with the winner receiving a four-year scholarship to Colorado Women's College.

Behind each PC award is a story of the dividends that faith and good will can pay. The winners of the President's Trophy which is presented to the "Handicapped American of the Year" are people who exemplify the ingenuity and imaginative vigor of America. One of them, Anne H. Carlsen, Ph.D., of Jamestown, North Dakota, is described by her admirers as the "completely adjusted handicapped woman."

Dr. Carlsen was born with only stubs of arms that ended above the elbow. One leg ended above the knee and the other was malformed, terminating in a clubfoot. At four, her mother died. Her father, Alfred Carlsen, and a thirteen-year-old sister gave every encouragement to the little girl and soon she was playing games with the rest of the children and even managed to participate in an amended version of baseball with the assistance of a coaster wagon. Hers was a hard uphill struggle including a long siege in a hospital to straighten contractures of her knees. This done, she was fitted with artificial legs and soon learned to use crutches. She developed amazing dexterity with the stumps of her arms and managed to write a beautiful hand. She even passed her driver's test and was able to drive a car.

After she took charge of the Crippled Children's School in Jamestown, Dr. Carlsen developed an international reputation for her genius in rehabilitating extremely handicapped boys and girls. Numbers of severely impaired students have left the school each year, thoroughly trained for social independence. Many went on to college and graduate school —inspired by the noble example that Dr. Carlsen had set.

All through history there have been temporary and permanent handicaps in a great variety of forms.

One August issue of "Performance" warned: "Watch that sunburn. It handicaps!"

In a guest editorial, Secretary of Agriculture Orville Freeman paid his respects to some immortal geniuses who had suffered disabilities, but not in vain: "From Demosthenes to Franklin Delano Roosevelt, the ability of the handicapped to make outstanding contributions to society has time and again been strikingly demonstrated. The biographies of the great men of history reveal that a surprisingly large proportion had major physical handicaps. Homer and Milton were blind, Moses and Demosthenes reputedly had defects of speech, Beethoven and Edison were deaf, Keats and Mozart—early victims of tuberculosis . . . It has been said that Franklin Roosevelt's crippled legs made him a humanitarian; Beethoven's growing deafness has been called 'the preparation for the flowering of genius.' And certainly Milton's blindness did not dim his poetic vision in the writing of 'Paradise Lost.' "

Coming up through history to the present, Secretary Freeman wrote: "Nature has a way of compensating for the handicaps which afflict the human body—I know from experience. It is in this light that we must view the physically handicapped of our time . . .

"There are many jobs in agriculture and in food processing and marketing for which handicapped men and women are extremely well qualified. As Secretary of Agriculture, I will do everything in my power to see that the handicapped have full opportunity to fill these jobs. This I firmly believe is not only in the best interests of the nation; it is an expression of faith in democracy itself."

Secretary Freeman was an authority on rehabilitation. Serving as a young Marine officer in the South Pacific during most of World War II, part of his jaw was shattered during combat action on Hollandia. There were operations and plastic surgery, and a painful period during which his mouth was wired shut. Finally, he had to spend six months learning to talk again. After that, he took his law degree and went on to become Governor of Minnesota and Secretary of Agriculture.

Millions of Americans, including Thomas Edison, have not allowed deafness to cripple their ability to perform. For most of this century, the Firestone Tire and Rubber Company has had an outstanding record of employing deaf workers to operate huge punch presses, perform chemical laboratory experiments, set type in the printing department, work on production of rubber goods, and in many other occupations.

Another striking example is the "stock exchange story," starring Patricia Melton and Wanda Thompson. In 1957, the two girls became "the best board markers" that the brokerage firm of Merrill Lynch Fenner & Beane ever had. Because of their lack of hearing, the girls were able to concentrate despite the many distractions of a brokerage office. They had to learn the code letters for the 300 stocks—which are different from the standard listing—and be able to record the accompanying figures on the board as they went "whipping by" on the screens.

Chapter Twenty

Always on "Active Duty"

The Maas family had moved to Essex Avenue in Chevy Chase, Maryland, but Mel again had his "office" arranged the way he wanted it.

After he realized that there was something dramatic about a blind man's adventures in a sighted world, he had a great idea for a book with a self-explanatory title—"Soup With a Fork." Perhaps he enjoyed talking about it more than actually writing it, but he worked on it whenever he could.

By 1963, the immediate family had shrunk to a threesome. In addition to the General and Mrs. Maas, tall young Joe was at home when he wasn't busy with college activities. After being a "drop-out" when he enlisted in the Marine Corps, Joe went to the University of Maryland where he was on his way to being graduated magna cum laude.

A "New York Times" reporter, Martin Tolchin, dropped around to interview the General for an excellent story that was published on April 8, 1963.

Among other words of wisdom, Mel told Mr. Tolchin, "The handicapped who've made a readjustment are the best adjusted people in the world. In order to overcome a handicap, a person must learn to look at himself and adjust to himself, something that most persons never learn."

The "Times" story brought the history of the three Maas daughters up to date. It stated, "They are Patricia, a Major in the Marine Corps; Mrs. Lee Catterton, an occupational therapist, and Mrs. Anthony Martino." I later told Sandy—Mrs. Anthony Martino—that I was indignant about her "unclassified status" in that paragraph. On behalf of motherhood, someone should have mentioned that she was busy rearing four attractive youngsters—with baby Robbie soon to make it five!

Mel and Katherine Maas had six grandchildren at that time. The Cattertons were the parents of two lovely little daughters. Mr. Catterton is in the automobile business.

Mr. Tolchin's story noted that the General spent three days a week in the office down on Constitution Avenue and kept in daily touch with his staff through tape recordings. He was still setting a "whirlwind pace." As Chairman of the President's Committee, he had logged more than 800,000 air miles, including nine trips abroad.

The General's health was in an even more precarious state that year. Arthritis had stiffened his fingers until they were badly gnarled. Because his feet were too numb to register pain in time, his toes were often bruised from colliding with furniture. He laughed at the idea that he had reached "the bedroom slipper age" for good, but they did feel comfortable. His mouth felt better, too, without those blasted false teeth.

Any other great citizen would have been content to sit by the fire and bask in the memories of his achievements and honors. Mel Maas had trouble thinking of retirement as long as there was something worthwhile to do. The men of the Maas family do not take easily to "senior citizenship"—the older brother, Frank, owns the Alta Sierra Ranch at Clovis, California, and he is the busiest man on the place.

Even though Mrs. Melvin Maas was "not on the playing field" much of the time, she had a good view from the bleachers. Recalling all those years when Mel resembled a human dynamo, Katherine Maas commented recently, "My husband, with his searching mind, had a way of stimulating people to use their talents to the utmost. His ever-present enthusiasm was an important factor too—his infectious sense of humor a delight—his way of speaking an inspiration to all who heard him."

All those noble traits were in evidence when General Maas went to keep a date in the Rose Garden at the White House on November 7, 1963. He no longer had a head of curly hair, and he looked quite frail. Even though they didn't show, he was wearing bedroom slippers on his sore, bruised feet. Still, it was a gala occasion for him, with every moment to be savored.

Those November moments were more precious than anyone knew. There was an almost spiritual tinge to the visit because General Maas was presenting the new Seal of the President's Committee—with the word "Physically" stricken out—to the President of the United States.

The dramatic scenes in the Rose Garden are on film in the offices of the President's Committee. Among those present were about seventy-five state chairmen and secretaries who were in Washington for a training workshop.

It was natural that General Maas should enjoy the Irish charm and wit of the tall young man who graced the highest office in the land, and he was warmed by the sincerity of his informal remarks as he welcomed the visitors and said, "We appreciate what you are doing in the states . . . This is a matter of great interest to all of us."

In subsequent comments he noted that a "giant step ahead" had been taken, in the effort to achieve equality of consideration for all the handicapped: "We are now working particularly hard . . . on the hiring of the mentally retarded, here, and all over the Government. The Civil Service Commission, with the cooperation of the various departments of the Government, is giving this particular attention.

"We also have a program here for those whom we regard as mentally restored, those who pass through a difficult period but who are fully capable of carrying their burden. In addition, as you may know, the Civil Service Commission itself gives some of its tests in braille so that those who are blind may occupy a useful place in society . . . I hope we can do more in the national government, and I hope you will do more in your states. I hope private industry and labor will also realize that those who are handicapped frequently are more than compensated by their desire to be useful and play a gainful role."

He emphasized the importance of trying "to develop a climate in this country where there is as close to full employment as we can get it," which would mean that there would be more jobs for the handicapped. He even included "men adrift"—the victims of technological change in coal mining sections of the country. "This," he said, "is not directly in your area of responsibility, but it is still tied into those who have been handicapped in one way or another."

As he stepped forward to present the large, handsome Seal of the "President's Committee on Employment of the Handicapped," General Maas saluted the young President for his strong, progressive leadership in broadening the field of employment for the handicapped. Government cooperation was setting an example for private industry, he declared.

During the moment of small talk that followed, the President threw back his head and laughed heartily. General Maas had reminded him of some World War II legislation in which he had been involved. "You wouldn't be here today if I hadn't sponsored the purchase of those PT boats from England," Mel said with a mischievous grin. "That's where you got your fame!" He was referring to the widely acclaimed heroism of PT Boat Commander John F. Kennedy when his craft was sunk in the South Pacific.

The tall, handsome President was scheduled to appear in Dallas later that month. The assassination, on November 22, came as a shocking blow to General Melvin Maas. He had developed a fond respect for the Chief Executive who shared his own concern for the neglected and the victims of prejudice. President Kennedy, too, had known pain and disability, and he was kindred to the people who live on the other side of the window in another world—the Land of Empty Hours. For him, understanding and sympathy were not enough. Something could be done—and would be done—to bring even the mentally retarded into some mainstream of life. In addition to all that, as Major Patricia Maas pointed out, "There is a special bond between men who have served in Congress. It rises above partisanship."

William P. McCahill noted, "In retrospect, the 2 years, 10 months, and 2 days of the Kennedy Administration were rich in blessings for the handicapped of America." It was gratifying to observe that President Lyndon B. Johnson and Mrs. Johnson, and Vice President Hubert H. Humphrey and Mrs. Humphrey, would become deeply committed to the same humanitarian problems.

General Melvin Maas, writing as Chairman of the President's Committee, sent out a typical message of New Year's optimism in 1964. He said in part: "As we glance backwards to our beginning, we can count perhaps six or seven million handicapped persons placed in employment despite their physical or mental disabilities. It is this collective feat that gives us the courage to continue our efforts. It is this remarkable accomplishment that gives strength to each of us, in his own way, to resolve that in 1964 we will help one more handicapped person to help himself through suitable work.

"If each of us accepts this challenge we will have a legion of citizens extending their efforts to advance the cause of their physically and mentally handicapped neighbors."

General Maas was back in Bethesda Naval Hospital several times during the winter, but the President's Committee published this heartening bulletin on March 20, 1964: "Hopefully, with the approval from his doctors, General Maas will attend the Annual Meeting on April 30." Vice Chairman Harold Russell would preside, and acceptances from President Johnson and former President Truman were awaited. Mrs. Lyndon Johnson was scheduled to open an exhibition of handicapped arts and crafts. There would be programs, panels, special speeches by great Americans. Mel's good friend, Dr. Frank Krusen, would act as toastmaster at the International Luncheon. It sounded as though it would be a festive, informative affair. Mel Maas always loved those Annual Meetings, and who—on heaven and earth—could say that he would not be there in 1964?

Ill as he was, Mel Maas was not about to give up. Over the years, the present Commandant of the Marine Corps had become familiar with the other man's special brand of vitality. Shortly after General Maas lost his eyesight in 1952, General Greene paid him a visit. The younger officer was amazed to see that there was "no attitude of blindness" about him. Mel Maas had kept the same energy, the same drive, the same dynamic interest in the programs that were dear to his heart. He walked back and forth in the room as though he could see. "It was almost as though he wouldn't admit that he was blind, or that he had become any different." General Greene paused reflectively. "He seemed to have one guiding thought in the back of his mind—that he was determined to live out a useful life."

In the spring of 1964, when the President's Committee was looking forward to seeing their Chairman at the Annual Meeting, General Greene visited General Maas in his hospital room at Bethesda. He found Mel Maas listening to a report about Congress on the radio and smoking a cigar as furiously as ever. He was brimming with the same mental energy that he had shown years before—with the same rejection of an "attitude of blindness." Said General Greene, "The fire still burned in him—the spirit was still driving him on." General Greene saw him as a "tremendous individual, with an undiminished interest in all the history-making programs he had helped to launch."

The Commandant recalled the Congressional Marine Breakfasts where Mel Maas drew people around him like a magnet. The membership includes all Marines and former Marines on Capitol Hill, and Mel was just as fond of the taxi drivers and janitors as of the Congressmen and officers. They were all Marines together, weren't they?

Early in April, the spiraling smoke of Mel Maas' cigar began to thin out. His tortured body, in its mortal weariness, pleaded for respite. But, even in an oxygen tent, General Maas was still himself.

Major Patricia Maas remembers that his restlessness lasted until the final moment, as though he kept thinking of so many things that still needed to be done. He had not been an obviously religious man, but he seemed to be listening intently for something. He grew quieter when the priest came and knelt with the family to pray. The reverential rhythm of the Rosary washed over the room, ". . . give us this day our daily bread . . . pray for us sinners now and at the hour of our death . . ." Halfway through the Rosary, Pat looked toward the bed and saw the restlessness fading from her father's face. At last he seemed content, serene.

The courageous heart stopped beating on April 13, 1964, exactly ten years to the day since General Maas had become Chairman of the President's Committee. Only a year before, he had been interviewed by Mr. Tolchin of the "New York Times." Only a few months before, he had been making witty remarks in the Rose Garden at the White House.

First among the tributes, on April 14, was the statement of the President of the United States, Lyndon B. Johnson, who lauded his former fellow Congressman:

"Not just the handicapped, but all the land grieves the passing of one of America's true heroes, Major Gen. Mel Maas.

"Blinded in the service of his country a decade ago, he taught himself a new existence without sight, traveled the world over, and inspired people everywhere about the capacities and abilities of the handicapped. Arthritis crippled his limbs and massive heart attacks limited his mobility; yet his spirit was whole; his spirit was never disabled.

"He has shown us how to live in the face of adversity. His courage and conviction have enriched us all. His spirit marches on, in us and in our land."

In the House Chamber where Congressman Melvin J. Maas had served so productively from 1927 to 1933 and from 1935 to 1945, Representative Albert Quie of Minnesota asked unanimous consent to address the House. He opened the floodgates of Capitol Hill oratory when he announced, "Mr. Speaker, it is my sad duty to inform the Members of the House of the death of a former colleague of many here and of a great American . . . It is to his credit and to the credit of his home state, Minnesota, that General Maas' activities throughout his life can be summed up under one general heading—'service to his country.' "

The hundreds of thousands of words that were uttered can, of necessity, be quoted only briefly here. One after another, the distinguished Members of Congress stood up to recall the dramatic vitality of the curly-haired young man who had come out of

Minnesota to speak his mind from the first minute. His close colleague and comrade, Mr. Carl Vinson of Georgia, summed up those many years of collaboration on the old Naval Affairs Committee with these words, "I can say with sincerity and conviction that he placed the security of the Nation before all other interests. Every member of the Naval Affairs Committee admired and respected his forthrightness, his integrity, his wisdom and his dedication to his Nation."

Next came the Speaker of the House, Mr. John W. McCormack, who had enjoyed "a pleasant chat" with the General at Bethesda Hospital the Sunday before. "His mind was keen. He knew who I was. He spoke with that fine candor he always had. I was very much surprised when I learned yesterday that he passed away so immediately after the visit I had paid to him on Sunday last . . ."

Some of the Congressmen mentioned just a few of the degrees and honors he had received—from St. Thomas College and Marquette University, from Presidents and Generals, from the Goodwill Industries, the Tri-Organization Scientific and Rehabilitation Conference, and veterans' and social welfare groups. It was also noted that he had led a "fourth" successful life, during which he had graced the boards of directors' tables in the United Services Life Insurance Company and Mutual of Omaha.

Mel Maas would have appreciated the note of humor that Mr. Charlie Halleck of Indiana injected amid the more somber recollections. "I cannot help but recall one personal experience I had with Mel many, many years ago," he said. "He used to go out to Anacostia and get one of the planes out there and fly. One evening he asked me to go along. Well, we had a great ride. He certainly demonstrated his ability. I think if I had known exactly what I was getting into, I would have stayed on the ground. But it was a great experience and one that I have always remembered very, very pleasantly . . ."

In one manner or another, all of his former colleagues bore witness to the statement of Mr. Leslie Arends of Illinois who noted that, "Mel Maas was more than a man of courage and ability. He was a man of compassion and understanding. His service to people went beyond his military service and beyond his congressional service. When he lost his sight he continued to serve his fellow men . . ."

Congressman Clark W. Thompson of Texas, who had "pushed papers and banged desks" alongside of his fellow-Colonel in the Marine Reserve office after World War II, believed that the passing of Mel Maas would "give rise to a great many reminiscences on the part of us oldtimers . . . Throughout the entire series will run the thread of fearless gallantry in action . . . To me, perhaps the outstanding demonstration of courage and gallantry came when he learned he was shortly to lose his eyesight. He was past fifty and had suffered a great deal of ill health. When the doctors told him what was in store for him, he made a typical comment: 'Well, I'd better get ready for it.' "

The last time that Mr. Clarence Brown of Ohio had seen Melvin Maas, he had been ill at Bethesda himself. He remembered Mel's greeting, "Where is that old devil from Ohio, Clarence Brown? I want to cheer him up a bit." Seating himself beside the bed, Mel told his friend, "Now don't worry about this thing. You will lick it. Look at me. They told me I would not last and here I am still going. There is a lot of work to be done by both of us. Keep your chin up—let's go."

Over in the Senate Wing of the Capitol, Majority Leader Mike Mansfield spoke of the "double bond" that had characterized his relationship with Melvin J. Maas: ". . . Mel Maas and I served together. While we were on opposite sides of the political fence, I always found him to be courteous, considerate, and tolerant. Both of us being ex-Marines, we, of course, had something more in common. On that basis, as well as others, a friendship developed which lasted during our lifetimes . . ."

Senator Hubert H. Humphrey, who would become Vice President in the fall, remembered Mel Maas both as a Congressman from his home state and as a great human being: ". . . His own personal handicap did not discourage him in his efforts to help others; in contrast, it stimulated his reserve energies to help others who were afflicted by similar handicaps . . . Mel Maas attended many gatherings in Washington after his affliction with blindness; yet I can honestly say that while his eyes could not behold that which was before him, his mind encompassed all . . ."

Senator Karl Mundt from Mel Maas' neighboring state of South Dakota, spoke of the General as ". . . a great American patriot who inspired literally hundreds of thousands of Americans, both blind and sighted, by his courage and ability, through the use of braille. He had an uncanny capacity to recognize voices and to know people. He would say, 'I can see you, Karl . . .' "

On that subject, Sen. Milward Simpson of Wyoming also said, ". . . I recall when he came to Wyoming to establish a commission for the physically handicapped. One of his favorite expressions was, 'Oh, I can see;' or he would say, 'I see.' "

Among the most lyrical of the Congressional eulogies was that of Senator Lister Hill of Alabama, whose tribute included these lofty phrases: "Although Melvin Maas was denied the light of day, he carried the light of heaven into the dark places. He brought to the physically handicapped, the mentally restored, and the mentally retarded hope, help, and the faith that removes the mountains and subdues the kingdoms. Melvin Maas will live in our history as one of our greatest humanitarians and noblest patriots."

The outpouring of more softly voiced tributes continued as General Melvin J. Maas lay at rest on the Wednesday after his death. They "visited" him in a steady procession to say farewell—the high echelon officers who were entitled to wear stars and bars on their shoulders and the enlisted men who remembered him from Guadalcanal and Okinawa, and the statesmen and waiters and taxi drivers, and the members of the President's Committee and staff. He lay "in state" in front of a wall blazing with floral tributes—this man who had loved to fuss with the dogwood and azaleas and spiraea on his lawn in Silver Spring.

Bill McCahill, who is so talented in the language of the Marine Corps, described the scene as General Maas—dramatic and appealing even in death—made his final triumphant appearance: "Flanking the flag-draped casket were two large vases of blood-red roses, flowers he favored, sent by 'the family.' In repose, in his Marine blues with boat cape turned back and two shining silver stars on each shoulder, he was still 'in command.' His rows of ribbons bloomed bright against the floral tributes, somehow outshining them. On his left pocket was the 'Pentagon Patch,' symbolic of the days he served on the Reserve Forces Policy Board and as a Special Adviser to the Secretary of Defense during the Korean War."

The Fort Meyer Chapel was crowded to capacity for the funeral on April 16, 1964. As General Maas had requested, his boyhood friend, Monsignor Patrick Ryan—a former two-star Army Chief of Chaplains—offered the Requiem Mass.

As the casket was carried out of the chapel by six young Marines in dress blues, a line of stalwart pallbearers stood at attention. Joe Bartlett, who was one of them, remembers those hours of farewell through a "hazy blur" of incredulity. In the illustrious "guard of honor" with Lieut. Col. Bartlett were General Wallace M. Greene Jr., General Alfred Gruenther, Colonel William P. McCahill, Charles Jordan, and old friend John Courtney from St. Paul—all men whose faces were etched somewhere in the book of Mel Maas' life.

Out into the spring sunlight, where a battalion of Marines stood stiffly erect, came Mrs. Maas, with Joe towering protectively over her, and the two "civilian" daughters in black, and Major Patricia Maas in her dress blues. The caisson with its black horses and flag-draped casket moved slowly toward the foot of a hillside in Arlington National Cemetery. Mrs. Maas had chosen an appropriate resting place for her husband. The strong young Marines carried the casket up the slope, and Monsignor Ryan spoke his final blessing.

The thirteen-gun salute thundered in the sweetness of an April noontime, and the three rifle volleys clipped the air. A few people might have heard a note of finality for General Melvin J. Maas in the fading echoes of "Taps." To the vast multitudes whose lives he had touched, he would always be a living legend—always on "active duty."

Chapter Twenty-one

To Set in Motion

Washington's tulips, forsythia and magnolia greeted the crowds from all over the country and overseas as they arrived for the Annual Meeting on April 30 and May 1. Mel Maas was there in spirit—in the tapping of white canes and crutches, the faint swishing of wheel chairs, the silent presence of braces and prosthetic appliances. He was there in the surges of animated conversation and in the sound of music as the Marine Band saluted the handicapped with Henry Stephen's "March of the Valiant."

President Lyndon B. Johnson was there, as were Secretary W. Willard Wirtz, News Commentator Howard K. Smith, President of the International Brotherhood of Electrical Workers Gordon M. Freeman, and a beaming host of distinguished guests and award winners.

Mrs. Melvin J. Maas was there, and the flame of her husband's presence glowed brightly as she said, "To all of you wonderful people assembled here, my grateful appreciation for the expressions of sympathy. They have been a true source of comfort to me and my children. They spoke of Mel as a source of inspiration. He spoke of you as his source of inspiration, with wonder and admiration for your giving of yourselves and your time in this great work. His affection for you was boundless and I want to thank you in his name."

Mrs. Maas also noted that, "In the last days of Mel's life he expressed to me his deep desire that you, Harold, would be named to succeed him. His wish has come to pass. I offer my sincerest congratulations to you. I know of no one of whom I could be prouder as Mel's successor."

It was Harold Russell who now stood in Mel Maas' place, calling him back to take another bow as he said, "At this precise point in the past ten Annual Meetings, Chairman Mel Maas would grope his way to this podium, feel for the microphone, pause for a long moment and—in a voice that really didn't need a microphone—proceed to speak as though he were chatting with each of us individually.

" 'Yes, I'm handicapped,' he would say—this man who was blind; who had arthritis so bad that his fingers couldn't 'read' braille; who had had several serious heart attacks, one right on this platform; who had hardening of the arteries and diabetes and ulcers, and I don't know how many other shattering ailments. 'Yes, I'm handicapped,' he would say; 'I wear false teeth.'

"And, even though we had heard his little joke many times before, we relished hearing it again. For it wasn't so much a joke as it was one man's personal testament of courage. We knew that if friend Mel could come out fighting each year, with a smile on his lips, so could we; so could we.

"He could not see us sitting before him, but he could open our eyes."

Harold Russell spoke of the difficult task of following in Mel Maas' path, but it was evident that "Somebody up there" loves the President's Committee when Chairman Russell finished his address with these sublime phrases: "Let the body or the mind be handicapped, but let the flame be free to burn brightly. This is the flame of civilization, the flame that makes us men and not animals, the flame that has given us peace and justice and kindness and mercy and love.

"When any man's flame is stifled by prejudice and misunderstanding and rejection, the whole world is the poorer. When any man's flame is allowed to burn brightly, the whole world is the richer.

"We have a stake in humanity. May God give us the courage and the strength to meet the challenge."

The superb human warmth, the sparkle, and the wit of Mel Maas would indeed be perpetuated in the person of Harold Russell.

The Annual Meeting was a tribute to the man who couldn't quite get there. The Executive Committee devoted the inside cover of the Minutes of the Meeting to this eloquent "In Memoriam" salute:

"The handicapped have lost a great champion;

and upon us, the living falls the task of carrying on as he would have wished.

"His path is not an easy one to follow. He brooked no half-victories, no easy ways out; he shirked no battles; he gave no quarter to the enemies, intolerance and injustice. He displayed infinite patience, and if he could not win a victory for the handicapped today, he would try again tomorrow and tomorrow; for he knew that some bright tomorrow, victory would come.

"He was courage personified. Disabilities, in his view, were not to be complained about, but to be surmounted. Blindness, heart condition, arteriosclerosis, diabetes, arthritis, and more—these could not stop him, for his spirit, his indomitable spirit, remained whole.

"His life on earth has been an inspiration, not just to the handicapped, but to all people. He taught us the most important lesson of our time—that adversity need not be a plague, but a challenge.

"Let each of us rise just a little taller to the challenges of life; and let this be our own personal tribute to the unconquerable spirit of our friend, our leader and our teacher, Major Gen. Melvin J. Maas, United States Marine Corps Reserve, Retired; Chairman of the President's Committee on Employment of the Handicapped for exactly ten fruitful years, April 13, 1954, to April 13, 1964.

"May his spirit guide us for all time."

His spirit does guide and inspire those who sustain his personality enriched ideals. The Blinded

Veterans Association and other organizations serving disabled persons are beneficiaries of the Major General Melvin J. Maas Memorial Rehabilitation Fund, which was founded less than a year after the death of the General. In addition to Mrs. Katherine Maas, who signed the incorporation papers, the members of the first Board of Directors are William P. McCahill, executive secretary of the President's Committee; Irvin P. Schloss, national vice president of the Blinded Veterans Association; the Honorable Mary Switzer, commissioner of Vocational Rehabilitation, Department of Health, Education and Welfare; the Honorable John S. Gleason Jr., administrator of Veterans Affairs; the Reverend Thomas J. Carroll, executive director of the Catholic Guild for All the Blind, Inc.; Kenneth C. Clark, national president of the Blinded Veterans Association; James F. C. Hyde, assistant director, Office of Legislative Reference, Bureau of Budget and a member of the Board of Directors of the Blinded Veterans Association; and Oliver C. Bacon, executive director, Blinded Veterans Association.

When President Truman proclaimed the first observance of National Employ the Handicapped Week in 1945, the demobilization floodgates had suddenly opened wide after World War II and millions of veterans—many with service-connected disabilities that would require rehabilitation training—were back home seeking jobs. Two decades later, General Maas' noble dream that the President's Committee would some day "go out of business" was no nearer reality. Scores of young American heroes were being brought back crippled and scarred from Vietnam. The "war of the highways" at home continued to be a scandal of major proportions. But General Maas would never admit defeat. He would scold and shake his head and try to joke as he went marching ahead, trying to bind up the wounds and lift the spirits of the victims of latter-Twentieth Century civilization.

The President's Committee is still very much "in business." The story of all the programs within programs—the vast humanitarian network of which the President's Committee is often the "nerve center" has barely been skimmed. One example may be found in an exchange of letters between Dr. N. Howard Hyman, president of the Jewish War Veterans Metropolitan Post No. 164 in New York City, and William P. McCahill. Dr. Hyman, who was a great friend of General Maas, wrote to Mr. McCahill about the remarkable work that was being done at the Castle Point Hospital at Beacon, New York, where fifty-six Vietnamese paraplegics are "the guests of our country." Dr. Hyman described the 1965 Christmas party sponsored by the local chapter of Paralyzed Veterans of America "where the foreigners were overwhelmed with kindness and friendship. A local group of men and women joined forces and gave out a great number of gifts. A patient of mine, a fine opera singer, flew in from his vacation and flew back the same night. He sang in French and they all loved his offerings."

Dr. Hyman spoke of drawing the Vietnamese patients into his delightful program of recreation and entertainment for the handicapped—which includes bringing small groups to New York for dinners, Broadway plays and concerts. It is possible to take much larger groups of handicapped veterans and nonveterans to sports events. "In fact, 1965, I believe was my most active year," wrote Dr. Hyman, "with many hundreds of wheel chair football fans attending all New York Giant home games . . ."

In his answer, Bill McCahill reported that "Harold Russell was extremely pleased when I told him what you are doing." Furthermore, a copy of Dr. Hyman's letter was being forwarded to the World Veterans Federation "as a matter of interest," and the President's Committee would broadcast the good news to other people who might be aroused "to go and do likewise."

When William McCahill testified before the Senate Subcommittee on Veterans Affairs, he delivered an inspiring presentation of all the reasons why the Veterans Administration Hospital in the District of Columbia should be named "The Melvin J. Maas Memorial Hospital." Among the most compelling were these: ". . . His life was lived for others. There is nothing in death that we can do for General Maas, but, even in death, General Maas can keep aflame the volunteer spirit in the breasts of those of us who remain and those who will follow in later generations." The bill has received strong support from many Congressmen who remember Mel Maas with affection—and from those who have often heard his legendary praises sung.

In the years since a young President was assassinated and mass murders have shocked the country, it reassures the fainthearted to look back to 1932 when a young Congressman coolly talked a demented gunman into dropping a loaded gun into his hand. Even then, he was "living his life for others."

The years have not dimmed the memories of those who knew Mel Maas. Among them is Senator Mike Mansfield. This author was granted the privilege of "calling" the Senate Majority Leader off the floor to talk about General Maas. As he pondered for a moment, Senator Mansfield's face wore the pensive expression that has endeared him to everyone who has seen him—in person or on television. He spoke of the importance of the Marine Corps in the life of General Maas. "He was a Marine in the true sense of the word every hour of his life." The Senator was profoundly impressed with Mel's strength of character in adjusting to his blindness—and then marching forward to take on the enormous responsibilities of the President's Committee on Employment of the Handicapped, to work for a better life for those who had suffered similar afflictions.

The Speaker of the House, John W. McCormack, continues to visualize his "late beloved friend" as "not only a great American, but an outstanding Legislator. Melvin Maas was not only a great man, but a good man. He was truly 'One of God's Noblemen.' "

It is obvious that General Maas has joined the host of the "invincible handicapped" who have proved throughout history that disabilities need not cripple the spirit. Although he could no longer speak for himself, the General was the "guest of honor" at the senior high school at Suitland, Maryland, on the afternoon of April 24, 1966. That was the day that Memorial Chapter 17 of the Disabled American Veterans changed its name to the "General Melvin J. Maas Chapter."

Through the courtesy of President Lyndon B. Johnson, the excellent martial music was furnished by the same United States Marine Band that performs for White House functions and seldom appears outside the Capital City. The Color Guard also was there, marching up the center aisle with ceremonial precision to present the Colors and retire the former flag of Chapter 17.

Wallace G. Daniel, the present Commander of Chapter 17, reviewed the history of the original Chapter which was chartered in 1948 by Jonathan M. Wainwright, hero of Corregidor and National Commander of the Disabled American Veterans, after he came home from World War II.

The words that were spoken that Sunday afternoon could fill a book. Speaker after speaker told of his memories of General Maas. All of them described him as a great patriot and an exhilarating human being. Colonel William P. McCahill told of the way he could appeal to the better natures of a whole roomful of people, because each one would have the feeling that he was speaking directly to him. Another old friend summed him up in a few gently spoken words: "He had a warm, generous personality—and a stiff spine." A sightless veteran recalled that they had both faced blindness together, and that Mel had talked him out of the depths of his despair.

In honoring General Maas, homage was often paid to the branch of service in which he took lifelong pride. One veteran, who had finished college before he enlisted in the Marine Corps, recalled with a smile, "I thought I knew everything—until I got to Parris Island and met my Drill Instructor."

This was the world of General Melvin Maas. Almost everything was there—except the powerful fragrance of his cigar. Seated in the front row on the platform were General Maas' three daughters, his son, and his grandson Marty Martino. Both Major Patricia Maas and Melvin "Joe" Maas Jr., participated in the ceremonies, extending greetings from Mrs. Maas in Mexico and speaking with the ease and eloquence that have become a family tradition. Major Maas presented the new blue and gold "General Melvin J. Maas" flag to the Chapter on behalf of the family, and Joe reviewed the most significant highlights of his father's life and the influence of his philosophy on the history of the country, on his family—and on himself in particular.

Climaxing the ceremonies, a Marine bugler caught and held a moment of nostalgia with the first soaring notes of "Taps" as the assembled guests—the clergymen, veterans, military personnel, Maryland officials, a dozen members of the Maas family, and other interested persons—stood to face the east in a silent salute to those departed members who had fought and died for freedom with honor.

While Marianne Maas Catterton was "on stage," Mr. Catterton sat with their two delightful little daughters—Jenny, seven; and Cindy, five—in the front row. The Cattertons had driven over from Annapolis.

Joe's wife, Connie Haile Maas, was there with her parents, but they had left their dainty little daughter at home. Christine was not quite old enough to appreciate dedication ceremonies. Since his graduation from the University of Maryland, Joe Maas has been employed as a management intern in the U. S. Department of Labor.

Quite a few years ago, Grandfather Maas had taken his first grandson on his knee and had explained that blind people can actually get around and "see" a great deal. "I know," Marty Martino had exclaimed, "you can see with everything but your eyes!"

When he was at Suitland in 1966, Marty Martino was a dignified fourteen-year-old whose passion was cars—a contagious enthusiasm that he was passing on to three-year-old Robbie. In addition to Mr. Martino and Robbie, Marty and his mother were representing Kathy who was thirteen, Patti who was ten, and Judi who was eight years old in 1966. They all live in Richmond.

Because it is the destiny of a handful of perceptive mortals to set in motion gigantic forces that far outlive them, the spirit of Major Gen. Melvin Maas will never be "retired" from the Marine Corps. General Richard C. Mangrum has called him "the patron saint" of the Marine Corps Reserve.

Although the Reservists were not called up during the early part of the Vietnam conflict, many of them followed in Mel Maas' bootsteps as individual Marines who volunteered for active duty. Those who remained aboard their home bases were not idle. The "Sunday Punch"—as the MCR often is called—was poised and ready to swing into action beside the Regulars at any necessary time or place.

The Marine Corps Reserve celebrated its fiftieth birthday in 1966 with the grand mixture of solemnity and fanfare that is typical of the Leatherneck fraternity. Of particular interest was the publication of "The Marine Corps Reserve—A History, 1916-1966." Colonel William P. McCahill, USMCR, officiated as the "commanding officer" in compiling and editing all the fascinating facts and anecdotes that were contributed by a host of "MCR historians."

The presence of Mel Maas is much in evidence in the book, which is inscribed: "A tribute to Major General Melvin J. Maas, USMCR, and all other Reserve Marines who fought and died for God, Country, and Corps from 1916 to 1966."

The Foreword is written by General Wallace M. Greene Jr., who previewed its contents with these words: ". . . This Golden Anniversary edition covers the 50 crucial years from 1916, when Congress first authorized a Marine Corps Reserve, to 1966, when the 4th Marine Division/Aircraft Wing Team is an integral part of the muscle of American armed strength."

Postmaster General Lawrence F. O'Brien observed the occasion by issuing a commemorative five-cent stamp. Designed by Stella Grafkos, it pictures four marching Marines—a modern combat Marine, a frogman, a World War II pilot, and a World War I "devil dog." Behind them stands the figure of a Revolutionary War Marine. The stamp was issued during the colorful first-day ceremonies on August 29 at the Iwo Jima Monument—a high point in the Fiftieth Anniversary celebration.

The August issue of "Leatherneck" Magazine saluted the Marine Corps Reserve with a striking cover picture of the Reserve Medal, standing out against a white background. Inside the magazine was a lively six-page feature story, "MCR's First 50 Years," written by S/Sgt. Harvey Hall and illustrated by Leatherneck Staff photographers—plus a list of "Units of the Organized Marine Corps Reserve."

In another monthly story highlighting MCR activities, with handsome "Leatherneck" illustrations and text, the "weekend warriors" at Los Alamitos Naval Air Station were shown doing what Mel Maas loved to do—getting off the runway and into the sky. These men use supersonic jet aircraft for "navigation flights and bombing runs" over the desert, and "Helicopter pilots sharpen their skills by practicing rescue work with Marine and Navy pilots who volunteer to jump into the bay so they can be picked up."

During the Korean war, "Chesty" Puller stomped up and down that war-battered land with his Marines, complaining about lack of coordinated air support. Now the Marines—both in Vietnam and at home—have their own "built-in" jet bomber squadrons and helicopters and their own sophisticated communications and radar systems. These are the Marine Air Wings for which General Maas fought so fiercely on Capitol Hill. Only for the benefit of future generations is it necessary to mention that the Leathernecks—on land and sea and in the air—lived up to their dynamic historical reputation in the Vietnam conflict.

The fighting men of the Marine Corps, both Regulars and Reserves, know that war is not an end in itself. As Commandant Wallace M. Greene Jr. wrote in the Foreword to "The Marine Corps Reserve—A History, 1916-1966": "The Marine Corps Reserve of today, like his father in World War II, his brother in Korea, or his grandfather in World War I, knows that the Marine Corps exists for a greater purpose than to kill or destroy. Reserves know that along with our military action we are building peace where there has been no peace, security where it hasn't existed and order where there is no order."

In their civilian lives at home, Reserves are building peace, security and order. In addition to training and educational programs, Marine Reserves have been active on the home front in civic service and human welfare programs. The "Toys for Tots" program is national; it would be impossible to list all the local community activities that they undertake, including emergency rescue services during floods and other disasters.

As General Greene noted, during an interview at Marine Headquarters, General Maas has "stepped back," and the younger men are carrying on. The Commandant spoke of all the up-to-date educational equipment, including taped material, that is now being used for Marine Officer training. There are twelve hundred high schools with ROTC programs, and ten of them are now Marine Corps units, with Marine officers and "D.I.'s." These young people, as well as the units of National Young Marines who are sponsored by the Marine Corps League, are wearing forest green utilities and taking pride in Marine Corps traditions and discipline.

When General Greene inspected the Marine ROTC unit at Jesuit High School in New Orleans, he said the young men looked so sharp and alert that he found himself thinking of them as regular Marines—until he suddenly remembered that they were fourteen-year-olds!

Major Patricia Maas, who was present during that meeting with General Greene, had just returned from the 1966 National MCROA Convention, where she was unanimously elected National Secretary. An officer in the "Regulars," Pat has become the honored recipient of her father's lifetime "Number One" position on the Marine Corps Reserve Officers membership list. She told General Greene that the Reserves at the Convention spoke with warm appreciation of the personal support that he has so often given to them.

On a spring day, when the magnolia trees and tulips bloomed in Washington and the President's Committee was preparing for another Annual Meeting, Lieut. Col. Patricia Maas and I climbed the slope of Pershing Hill in Arlington National Cemetery. It was a splendid resting place for a restless Marine General, with a clear downhill view of Marine Headquarters. More distantly glimpsed, on the far side of the Potomac, were the Capitol and the Lincoln Memorial and other landmarks of the city that Mel Maas knew so well, even without his eyesight.

There are some elaborate monuments in the cemetery, but Pershing Hill is crowned with the simple, traditional headstones that symbolize the warmth of comradeship between certain officers and the more than one hundred thousand enlisted men whose graves mark the rolling green acreage at Arlington. That, Patricia Maas noted, was the request of General John J. Pershing, who commanded the two million American soldiers who fought in World War I—"a quiet hill and a simple headstone." His grave is near that of General Maas, who so often talked about equality—two great men whose burial plots are almost indistinguishable unless you search for them, and yet their deeds will stand as monuments down through the generations.

With his sense of humor, Mel Maas might have chuckled at the thought that he—a young Marine recruit in World War I—should finally rest in the upper echelon company of famous "Black Jack Pershing."

It was a crisp day, with a brisk wind blowing over Pershing Hill. A jet zoomed overhead, gathering altitude. With only a scattering of clouds, visibility was infinite. We could almost hear Mel Maas saying, "Oh, it's a great day for flying—let's go!"

Credits

Quotations from **One More Career for General Maas** by Richard and Gladys Harkness, March, 1956 Reader's Digest.

Leatherneck Magazine: Quotations from **Los Alamitos Reservists**, Jan. 1966; **MCR's First 50 Years,** August 1966; verse from "The Ballad of Iwo Jima" by Captain T. M. D'Andrea, September 1966.

Innumerable quotations from "Performance" magazines, News Letters, Minutes of Annual Meetings, and a variety of publications from the offices of the President's Committee on Employment of the Handicapped.

Quotations from **General Sets Example for Disabled He Aids** by Martin Tolchin, April 8, 1963 New York Times.

Quotations from **The Marine Corps Fights for Its Life** by Richard Tregaskis, Feb. 5, 1949 Saturday Evening Post. Quotations from **Don't Pity Us Handi-**

capped, by Melvin J. Maas as told to Paul Healy, Sept. 5, 1959 Saturday Evening Post.

Verse from "Architectural Blocks in School Buildings," published by the Illinois Commission for Handicapped Children.

Quotations from front page "big story"—**Maas Disarms Gunman Menacing House** by Alfred D. Stedman, Dec. 14, 1932 St. Paul Pioneer Press.

Quotations from **Blind General Maas Doesn't Consider Himself Handicapped; Shows, Tells Why** by Alan Levy, April 24, 1963 Louisville Courier-Journal.

Quotations from **How NOT to Help the Blind** by Major Gen. Melvin J. Maas, published originally in the American Legion Magazine, reprinted September 1963 by The President's Committee on Employment of the Handicapped.

Quotations from **Marine! The Life of Chesty Puller** by Burke Davis, copyright 1962 by Little, Brown and Company, Inc. Used by permission.